Contents Under PRESSURE

30 YEARS OF RUSH AT HOME & AWAY

MARTIN POPOFF

ECW PRESS

Published by ECW Press
2120 Queen Street East, Suite 200, Toronto, Ontario, Canada M4E 1E2
416-694-3348 / info@ecwpress.com

NATIONAL LIBRARY OF CANADA CATALOGUING IN PUBLICATION DATA

Popoff, Martin, 1963–
Contents Under pressure : 30 years of Rush at home & away / Martin Popoff.

ISBN 978-1-55022-678-2
ALSO ISSUED AS: 978-1-55490-678-9 (PDF); 978-1-77090-141-4 (EPUB)

1. Rush (Musical group) 2. Rock musicians—Canada—Biography. 3. Rock musicians—
Canada—Interviews. I. Title.

ML421.R952 P82 2004   782.42166'092'2   C2004-902838-3

Cover photo, research, & editing by Andrew MacNaughtan

Contributing photographers: Fin Costello, Andrew MacNaughtan,
Deborah Samuel, Dimo Safari, Philip Kamin, Bruce Cole & MRossi

Cover, Text Design, and Production: Tania Craan

This book is set in Joanna and Coniption

The publication of *Contents Under Pressure* has been generously supported
by the Canada Council, the Ontario Arts Council, the Government of Canada
through the Book Publishing Industry Development Program.

Printing: Marquis
7 8 9 10
PRINTED AND BOUND IN CANADA

ECW PRESS
ecwpress.com

Table of Contents

Introduction

Greetings, O Prog Rock Heads of Discerning Taste (and, by the way, congratulations on having such peerless good instincts as to be reading this).

The whole purpose of the book you now hold in your hands is, most obviously, to celebrate Rush's 30 years on their idiosyncratically own road to rock. This is not the official biography — more living, breathing, writing, recording, touring, tennis and night volleyball necessitate the generation of chapters not writable at this time — nor is it an exhaustive history of, well, anything.

What it is, however, is a pendulum-swinging firsthand account from the boys, a sort of oral history, of the accursed record-tour spin cycle (rinse 'n' repeat) that so many bands find the death of them. Rush came close to something between dissolution and implosion on many occasions, although the intensity of the drama surrounding such moments might not stack up to that of wilder road-rocking tribes. Yet, as you can see from the number of records crafted and tours logged, the band has indeed avoided any sort of official towel-throwing, gamely staying in the game for 30 years as of this juncture, 35 if you count the knockabout days before the hirsute, busty and bustling first album.

In essence, the goal here is to retain the lively, live-loving feel of a tour book, with the added bonus of a fair bit of commentary on the records. After all — and the guys in the band would agree — the real creativity, and the biggest rush of accomplishment, come with the writing and construction of the songs in the first place. As well, given that this is a band that purposefully plays an uncommon amount of any given new record on its subsequent tour, the album's role in setting the tone for the tour is singular. I should also mention that, toward the end of this tome, the guys spend a lot of time talking about the live situation in generals, abstracts and universals (granted, we had two triple live albums and a DVD to address) or, perhaps more specifically, as it exists today, with respect to the last tour, which is after all most relevant, save for the new one. Also most relevant is having the band expound at great length on the latest studio record, **Vapor Trails**. After all, for a set of minds furtively on the move outside and up the road, that album is closest to where Rush is now. And, no surprise, they really like it.

It was gratifying to me putting together this thing, first off because Alex, Geddy and Neil have not lost their memories of events, nor their understated, backhanded sense of humor (despite considerable tragedy among their ranks), nor their enthusiasm for what they've done and have yet to do. As caution, the reminiscences enclosed do not bear much resemblance to those of Led Zeppelin, Aerosmith, Motley Crue or even fall-about tourmates UFO, Thin Lizzy or (God forbid) . . . Wild Horses. Instead, what patterns itself out of the evidence, after one peers into the workings of roughly 20 albums and tours (depending on how one counts), is that Rush took the task at hand seriously, studiously, extending that credo to the act of surrounding themselves with good help who quickly became fast friends. Indeed, the road crew, led by Liam Birt and Howard Ungerleider, have for years been known as one of the best in the business. Indeed, many of them have been around virtually as long as Rush has been a band.

But for me, one of the more interesting areas of investigation was discovering all the bands that Rush had played with over the years, as backup to or headliner o'er. When it wasn't up to them, Rush found themselves with the cream-of-the-crop dream teams of '70s rock. Once it was theirs to point fingers and appoint, the band was known for championing cutting-edge music and even solo musicians they themselves appreciated. Whether it was from hard rock, new wave, progressive rock proper, avant garde or courageous pop, Rush was there with red-carpet support (soundchecks, booze, encouragement), proposing well-reasoned listening recommendations for your lighter-foisting, Limelight-loving self.

It was also interesting for me to see where emphasis was put in terms of tour circuitry. As the years ground on, one could sense patterns in where the pullback starts and which territories were first to see a reduction of face time. The intensity of forethought on the subject is debatable, but the tour history reveals a philosophy, almost an alternate personality of the band, or more accurately a clue about its composite personality. The words *balance, deliberation* and *peace* come to mind, maybe even *peace and quiet,* maybe even *quietude.*

So, in any event, congratulations to the boys for keeping their wits about them all these years, for inspiringly carving out rich lives and, indeed, for something as simple as illustrating good grace under pressure in front of those privileged enough to tour with them.

Martin Popoff

Early Days

The early history of what can arguably be called Rush is actually quite a long one, reaching back a good five years before that first wollopingly Zeppelinesque album on Moon Records. At times a four-piece with a revolving door of players, the band wouldn't actually become something worthy of the tag "the grandfathers of progressive metal"(!) until well past Neil Peart's arrival, until, that is, the three amigos committed their special purpose to wax with a little something called Fly by Night As alluded to in the introduction, this book is neither the time nor the place for a detailed history of the band, but it is indeed a celebration of the art, science and sheer luck of constructing records and playing live. In that spirit, I offer a few words from Alex Lifeson (born Alex Zivojinovich), Geddy Lee (born Gary Lee Weinrib) and Neil Peart (just born, but not really as a drummer — that took 13 years) on the formative years, when pushing air to small tribal gatherings was all they had to confirm their very existence.

"Well, let's see, we started in September of '68," begins Alex. "We got a gig in a United Church basement where they had a drop-in center on Friday nights. We played this gig, and we knew maybe seven or eight songs — mostly Cream and Hendrix — and we would just play them over and over, repeatedly throughout the night. And through the rest of the week, we would get together and rehearse and learn more songs.

"We started writing right from the beginning; I think we wrote our first song within a few months. The first original song we wrote was called Losing You, and it was kind of an up-tempo bluesy thing.

"And we continued doing that gig pretty much on a weekly basis until the spring of 1969. The first gig we played there, there were probably 30 people. By that spring, there were about 200, 250 people. I mean, the place was packed! And we had two solid sets of material, and that was a real treat; it was so exciting."

World domination was drafted, says Alex, shortly thereafter. "We got ten bucks to do that first gig. And we went to Pancers, a deli at Steeles and Bathurst; the gig was in that area, ten minutes from there. And we talked about, you know, what we were going to do now, where were we? [laughs]. At what level were we in the world of rock bands? We figured we were like number 10,680, even though we only knew a few songs [laughs]. But it was so exciting sitting in there. I can still visualize what the place looked like and the booth we were sitting in and how excited we were.

"And by the spring, we were getting 35 bucks a week to do that gig. So it was quite a big increase. And then we started playing high school dances, other drop-in centers, things like that. We continued doing that for the most part until '71, I guess, when they lowered the drinking age to 18. And then all of a sudden there were all these bars you could play in.

"We went through some difficult periods. You know, John Rutsey [drummer on debut album and part of first tour] had some health issues. So there were a few times when things kind of just went into limbo. We had some changes in the lineup a couple of times. Joe Perna was the bass player for a little while; Geddy was gone for a bit, and then he came back. Geddy's brother-in-law played in the band in the spring of '69 for a few months, playing piano and guitar. We were still playing a lot of bluesy stuff. Mitch Bossi came later [lasting February to May of '71]. But Lindy Young was in the band for a little while, and then he quit [Young was in from January to July '69]. Mitch came in I think just as we were doing the bar gigs; he might have done a few of the bar gigs."

Legend has it that Rutsey's older brother just blurted out the name Rush one day, and it stuck. But along the way, the band had been called Hadrian (not bad), and Geddy had been in bands such as Ogilvie and Judd (ok, those ain't so hot). Very early on, Lactic Acid's Jeff Jones was also part of the stew.

Geddy sifts the sands and recalls a few of the covers Rush used to conjure up through the early '70s. "We did a version of For What It's Worth; we

Toronto Musicians' Association
LOCAL No. 149
AMERICAN FEDERATION OF MUSICIANS OF THE UNITED STATES AND CANADA

used to do this old Motown song called *Roadrunner*, but it didn't sound anything like *Roadrunner*; I don't know why we called it *Roadrunner*. We made it into this long extended jammy thing; Alex used to play a really long solo, but of course they were all like that. Earlier we used to play *Crossroads*, *Suffragette City* by David Bowie. I don't know if we ever played Zeppelin in the bars. I know when we were just a high school band we used to play *Livin' Lovin' Maid*. In the early, early days, we used to play Jeff Beck's *Let Me Love You*, from *Truth*. Also *Morning Dew*, some Yardbirds songs like *Shapes of Things*." Larry Williams' *Bad Boy* (made popular by the Beatles) got some airtime, actually right up until December '74.

"Certainly Zeppelin were the biggest influence at the time," adds Alex. "But, you know, so was Cream, Hendrix, John Mayall, Jeff Beck."

From the basement band days through the break of the new decade, other acts Rush (and pre-Rush) would cover included the Stones, Eric Clapton, Ten Years After and Traffic. Original compositions, such as *Keep in Line*, *Morning Star*, *Child Reborn*, *Love Light*, *Slaughterhouse* and *Feel So Good*, would also emerge. All the while, Alex scraped a little extra cash together by pumping gas and working with his dad, a plumber. Geddy worked in his mom's variety store.

If there can be said to be a fourth member of Rush, that would have to be manager and business overseer Ray Danniels, who has been with the band since early 1969 (of note, another longtime loyal trooper is Liam Birt, first hired on in '72 as lighting and guitar tech, now cracking the whip as tour manager). In the ensuing years, Ray would be associated with bands as big or bigger than Rush, including Queensryche and Van Halen, but many of those ties have been severed, with his friendship and inextricable business ties with Rush remaining.

"Well, he was a kid," says Alex, with respect to first meeting Ray, who had approached the band with a proposition at one of their high school gigs, having been familiar with them from their packed shows at The Coff-In. "I mean, we were 15 years old, and Ray was 16 years old. He left

home, I guess about a year earlier. He moved to Toronto, moved into Yorkville when it was a hippie hangout, hooked up with some people. There was a band called Sherman Peabody. Greg Godovitz was in the band then, and Ray used to live in their basement; he would sleep on the mattress in their band house in Willowdale. And I don't remember how we met, some common friend.

"After a while, Ray said, 'Listen, do you guys want a manager? I'd like to manage the band.' And of course he had no skill or experience, but he was a hustler. So he started managing us and set up some gigs and got posters and drove around on a friend's motorcycle putting posters up on telephone poles across the city, all that stuff.

"And eventually Ray just became more of a promoter; he started promoting other bands, and then he started an agency (Music Shoppe), and then that agency grew. So he was set very early on, in terms of where he wanted to go, in a business sense musically. And our relationship has existed since then."

Alex draws us back to re-create the sense of blinding glamour that enveloped the band on their earliest road trips. "I remember doing a gig at the Thunderbird Motor Inn in Thunder Bay, in October of '73. It was freezing cold. They had us at the far end of the motel. There was no heat down there; the rooms were around 50 degrees. Every night you would hear 'zzzzzzz' as we would turn the hair dryers on under the sheets to keep warm. And the guy wouldn't pay us after the first week. And we didn't have any money, so we had to eat and drink in his restaurant, and one night I remember he sat us down and said, 'Come on, boys, we're going to have some drinks.' We had all these drinks and had a great time, and . . . we got the bill for it! He actually gave us the bill for it [laughs]. But we had a real fun time up there back then.

"I remember doing a gig at The Meat Market. It was the old Colonial Tavern, on Yonge, right across from The Eaton Centre. It was a jazz club, but downstairs they had a rock club. And you can imagine, being in that location, what kind of crowd they brought in. And I remember I had surgery; I had my wisdom teeth taken out. And we were there doing the gig; I was 18, 19. And I was sitting on a chair on stage, because I was on Percodan, and my mouth was killing me, and I had smoked some hash. And this fight breaks out. And, like, every person in the place is in this fight, and it's all happening right in front of me, while I'm sitting in a chair playing, and I just remember looking at Geddy and him looking at me, like, 'What is going on?!' And we're playing a song called *You Can't Fight It* on top of it all."

You Can't Fight It actually figures prominently as Rush's first original recording, backing Buddy Holly's *Not Fade Away* on what is now a very collectible seven-inch single on the band's own Moon Records. *Garden Road* and *Fancy Dancer* were the other (latest) Rush originals that never made the grade. "Yeah, they were sort of riffy songs," says Alex, "very repetitive, mostly 12-bar sorts of things. They wouldn't have survived the test of time, I don't think."

"John had juvenile diabetes, and that was an issue in what he wanted to do," says Alex, offering a concise history of John Rutsey's time in the band as drummer. "John and I were friends from about the time we were 11. We would play hockey in the street. We were really interested in music, and that's all we cared about; he played drums, and I played guitar, and we used to have little bands, and you would play parties mostly. There was no money or anything, but somebody was having a party, and you would set up your equipment in their basements, and you would play some songs.

"John was a very funny person. He was really hip and cool; at least that's what we thought at the time. He was a great guy to hang around with, but he also had a dark side to him. But he got really sick at that time, and we started auditioning other drummers and just playing with some other people. But he came back, and then when the prospect of signing this deal came up with Mercury — the tour, all of that — he got scared, I think, of the whole thing. And it wasn't for him."

Rush

But John Rutsey would indeed be around for the recording of the pressing and impressionable self-titled first album, along with a handful of dates in promotion of it.

"Back then there wasn't a lot of time for a lot of takes," recalls Alex, with respect to the construction of what is emphatically the odd man out of the Rush catalog. "I remember, when we recorded the record the first time, we were playing The Gasworks. And we would finish the gig at 1:00 a.m., pack up the gear, and go to Eastern Sound. It was at Bay and Yorkville, but it's a parking lot now. And we would go in after hours and record from about two until nine in the morning, when their regular sessions would come in. And the reason we did that is that we got the studio at quarter rate or something; it was very, very cheap.

"It was all eight track back then. We went in one day, basically did all the beds. We'd been playing the songs for a long time, so it was just a matter of getting the sounds up and recording them and then coming back the following day to do overdubs and vocals and things like that. And that's why it took a couple of days to do. Terry Brown came down to see the band at The Gasworks a couple of times and came in to really save the project. *Finding My Way, Need Some Love* and, I think, *Here Again* were the songs that we rerecorded for the record. So we dropped *Not Fade Away, Can't Fight It,* and there may have been another one. All of this stuff we had been playing for one to two years before. *Working Man* we had been doing for a while; *In the Mood* was probably at least two years old, if not three, when we recorded the first record.

"And the whole first part of the recording experience was awful. We worked with this guy named David, who was working at our office; I'm not sure what his position was. We used to go and just hang out. He was from England, a nice enough guy and everything, and he had an engineering background, but he did such a horrible job. We spent two nights recording the entire record, and he mixed the whole thing in two hours. The drums were out of phase, and I think they were recorded on just two tracks. Things were missing, the sounds were awful, and it was just a real mess.

"And as I said, we dropped a few of the songs we had recorded, did three or four newer ones with Terry and basically repaired all the problems we had. I may have rerecorded some guitar stuff. We knew the songs so well that it was easy to fly through it. We spent a day or two with him,

and then he mixed it. So it was a real repair job that Terry did. He just breathed some life into it, and it was so much more what we thought it would be like, to work with him. Whereas David mixed it by himself; we did the thing and then had to leave — we kind of felt disconnected from it. And being the first record, it was so exciting. And so, of course, that was the start of that whole relationship with Terry that lasted through **Signals**."

As Alex explains, there was another interesting hurdle to overcome if Rush was to have their first album finished. "The funny thing is, John was the lyricist in the band at the time, and he wouldn't submit the lyrics for any of these songs. So Geddy had to quickly put some lyrics together for it. I wrote the lyrics on *Here Again*, but everything else was just sort of thrown together. And I think John probably regrets that, you know, to this day. There were the lyrics we were using for these songs live, but he didn't want them to be on the songs. It was just, like, 'Well, why?' 'I just don't.' 'Well, all right.' So they were a rush job, and it shows."

Geddy recalls things slightly differently. "We used to write the songs, and John would write lyrics. And sometimes he would say to us, 'I don't have them ready yet,' so I'd say, 'Well, I'll just make some stuff up. I'll just sing some off-the-cuff lyrics until you're ready with it,' when we were doing bars and stuff.

"So when it came time to record those songs that I'd been, you know, bluffing, coming into the studio I said, 'ok, where are the lyrics?' And he

said, 'Well, I didn't like them, so I tore them all up.' And I was supposed to start recording that day, start singing them. So I just sat down in the studio and started scribbling off lyrics and wrote as many as I could for the songs that we needed. And they ended up being the lyrics for those songs on the first album. It was all done over a period of two days, because we didn't have any lyrics. I don't know what was going on in John's head. All I knew is that I kept asking for lyrics, and he kept saying they were coming, and one day he said, 'I tore them up. They're not happening.' He was not . . . he had moments that were not strictly logical."

The above-cited problems did little to hamper the public's enjoy-

ment of the album. With riffs exploding everywhere, and with Geddy's unworldly yowl, **Rush** stood out as a high-tension proto-metal feast, screechingly insistent at a time when few dared rock this hard — especially in Canada, where up to this point Bachman Turner Overdrive and April Wine had served as the nation's benchmarks in hard rock. No less than *Finding My Way*, *What You're Doing*, *In the Mood* (sometimes said to be the first song Geddy ever wrote but perhaps more like his

first significant song) and *Working Man* — half the album — would last
long into the band's live sets. *Finding My Way* is the most Led Zeppelin-
like of the album's compositions, Geddy trying out the odd "ooh yeah"
over a drumless verse, while *What You're Doing* also pulverizes somewhat
Zep-like, housing the album's most combative celebrations of red-hot
riffery. *Need Some Love*, *Take a Friend*, *Before and After* and *In the Mood* are perhaps
a bit more dated, something closer to what UK or US boogie rockers of
the day might have written. However, it is lengthy, weighty, closer
Working Man that is, heads above, the album's classic, Geddy offering a
blue-collar tale similar in tone, or at least in its effect on crowds, to
Lynyrd Skynyrd's *Simple Man*.

    Rush was released on the band's own Moon label, after being rejected
by every label in Canada — this topic came up bitterly in interviews for
years, often with the story enlarging to the band having been turned
down by every label *twice*. The album was shortly thereafter rereleased on
Mercury upon signing. The US-based label had also snapped up Canadian
acts Bachman Turner Overdrive (not a lot of kind words from Geddy on
these guys) and Hammersmith and thus had a little niche established.
"The Moon copy was around for a little while," says Alex of the label
logistics. "Reviews? I can't remember if there were any. I want to say that
there weren't, because it just wasn't important enough. We were just a
bar band from the city, so you're not likely to get a review in the *Telegram*
back then or the *Star*. I know that it got some play on CHUM FM back
then. Dave Marsden played it; he used to play *Finding My Way*, *Here Again* and
I think *Working Man* before the rerelease, as the Moon record."

    Rush also had a product champion in Donna Halper from WMMS FM
in Cleveland, who gets thanked on the record for "getting the ball

rolling." *Working Man* was her weapon of choice, and the phone lines were summarily flooded, many fans under the impression they had just heard fresh Zeppelin music. A young Cliff Bernstein, then A&R for Mercury, was instrumental in getting the band signed (Casablanca almost got the nod), after which a hefty $75,000 advance came as part of a larger $200,000 deal.

Hitting the road, things quickly came to a head with John Rutsey. "We were placed to do this tour and go to America and all of what that meant," explains Alex, "but he backed out at that time. Plus also he wasn't really interested in where we wanted to go musically. Geddy and I were interested in bands like Yes, King Crimson and Jethro Tull. We wanted to move our music more into that progressive area, and he was more straight-ahead rock 'n' roll — Bad Company, that kind of stuff — which was more of a cross-section of what we were playing then in bars. So it was really time to go our separate directions."

And thus progressive metal was born. Which prompts a question: were the birthers themselves aware of the new arrival? "No, I think it was just something we wanted to do," proposes Alex. "It seemed right, you know? We liked to play hard rock, as a three-piece, but we wanted it to be more challenging, mostly musically, to ourselves.

"Neil was an unknown when he came into the band. We didn't know that he would be the lyricist that he would become. When he first auditioned, we spent a lot of time just sitting around and talking about music, literature and all kinds of stuff. We would play and then sit and talk, we'd play, sit and talk, and we spent the whole evening doing that."

Geddy adds that "months later we were on our first tour together, Alex and I suggested to Neil that because of all the reading he does and his obvious broader than average vocabulary, perhaps he might have a go at lyric writing. Alex and I certainly had no interest in the job. Neil was reluctant at first but said he'd give it a try. I think it worked out pretty well."

And thus Neil Peart, 21 years enthusiastic, joined the band on Geddy's 21st birthday, July 29th, 1974, amusingly supplanting his gig back home in a band called . . . Hush.

Neil recalls his whereabouts on the long days and nights before the one of which Alex speaks. "Well, I went to different auditions in '71, '72. I went to England, took my drums and records and went over there,

searching for fame and fortune. And the first thing I did when I got over there was get auditions out of the back of *Melody Maker* and the other music papers.

"I was soon getting disillusioned over there by the music industry, realizing it wasn't the way I thought it was. You didn't just get really good at the music you loved and become successful [laughs]. I was shocked, appalled, disappointed, disillusioned, all that. I also made the decision, well, if I can't make a living playing the music I like (at this point 18, 19), then I'll make a living some other way and still play the music I like. That became the point of honor. I think a lot of teenage musicians, if you decide to become a professional, you . . . decide to make a living playing music, no matter what. I grew up with guys who would play in polka bands and country bands; it didn't matter — they were making a living as drummers. Whereas to me, I would rather compromise [laughs] *myself*, and work for a living, and play in bands part-time that played music I liked. So that became the obvious choice for me.

"So at that time, when the Rush offer came along in the summer of '74, I was playing part-time in a band in bars and working all day in the family farm equipment business to make a living. As to how I would have continued? Probably like that. Playing music for love, and working for money [laughs]. That's the distinction."

I asked Neil about the competitive climate in the late '60s with respect to learning his craft — if it was anything like the instrumental study, dedication and intense competition Rush had almost single-handedly caused among the next generation of progressive metallers getting their first glimpses of their own potential mastery in the late '70s and early '80s.

"Well, I don't look at it in those terms," deflects Peart modestly. "But if you look at the late '60s, when I was doing my apprenticeship, what it took to be a rock drummer, from, say, 1965 to 1970 [holds his hands at a 45 degree angle], it elevated enormously, in terms of what you were supposed to be able to do. Just consider the difference. To be a drummer in 1965, all you had to do was play one beat. That's all you needed to know, nothing else. Whereas suddenly, through '67, '68, '69, what happened?! What it took to be a drummer was so daunting as a teenager at the time. 'That's what I have to do to be a good drummer?! I have to play

a complicated time signature, exotic percussion instruments, intricate arrangements, inventive drum fills?' All of that was coming at me as a teenager. That became my new benchmark, what you have to know to be a good drummer. That's the way I saw it.

"Again, it was all so innocent, in that I firmly believed as a teenager that all I had to do was to get good, and I would be successful. That was really my credo in the world. I thought it worked that way [laughs]. I was a kid.

"So I just pursued that goal, and through those years you'd start hearing different drummers come along — Phil Collins, Carl Palmer, Ian Paice, John Bonham — these people that really had technical ability. The music got really complicated and hard to figure out. The first time I heard somebody say 'This song's in seven,' I had no idea what they were talking about. So again that became something I had to learn; it had to become part of what I knew as a rock drummer. But I think there was a real change at that time that's never been equaled in the sudden growth of what the demands were. That happened in jazz, I suppose, as well."

"In the progressive rock period, Chris Squire and Jon Anderson were my idols," adds Geddy, mirroring a similar formative background to Neil's. "From that period, I used to admire all kinds of bass players. Jack Bruce was a real hero of mine; Jack Cassidy from Jefferson Airplane was a hero of mine. Plus Phil Lesh from The Grateful Dead; I used to like the way he played, the way he used to slink around the notes, throw in things. He would break away from the basic format, and I used to like these guys that stepped out, that stretched out a little bit. And once I started getting into some of the rock-jazz fusion stuff, Jeff Berlin was an influence on me; that was a bit later. He was playing with Bill Bruford's band. That's where I got introduced to his playing. In fact, we were working in London; I think we were recording at the time. They were playing a club, and Bill Bruford was a hero of ours from the Yes days. And when he started playing in his own band, we loved those first two records he did. They were tremendous, and Jeff was just a monster bass player, amazing."

"When he auditioned? He was really good," affirms Alex, with respect to the new recruit. "Neil hit his drums so hard. And they were a really small kit of Rogers — small toms, small bass drum and loud! He hit them hard. He played a lot like Keith Moon at the time. You can see in his playing where that would have come from. There was an energy in Keith Moon's playing, a constant movement. He never played time, Keith Moon. And I think that's basically where Neil got a lot of his fundamentals. Even today you can hear so much activity in his playing. It's subtler now, but it's always constant."

So was Neil so good that it was intimidating? "No, in fact, when he came in . . . he was working for his dad in a tractor business, farm tractor parts. So when he arrived for the audition [laughs] . . . first of all he sets up his tiny kit of drums, he's got really short hair, he looks a little bit like a boge, he's got the straight job, he's from St. Catharines. You know, we're from Toronto, we're cool, we've got long hair, leather pants, platform shoes and the whole thing. And I remember we thought, 'Is he going to look cool enough to be in our band?' I mean [laughs], that was one consideration at the time.

"But when he started playing, it was a real eye-opener. And we had such a common interest in music. And when we started playing, we really fed off each other, particularly Geddy and Neil. And that's where it starts from, the rhythm section, so if it clicked for them. . . . I think I was probably a little more hesitant. I don't know if I was so enthusiastic right off the bat. But I definitely warmed up to it quickly."

Alex said Neil was neither a wallflower nor a showman. "He wasn't nervous, and no, I mean, he would do some of his stick twirls, but that's about as showy as he got. But he just played so great and so powerfully; it was very different from John's style of playing. It really projected the band in a much more powerful way." Which was a fortuitous situation, considering that Neil's first show with the band was to 18,000 people, backing up Uriah Heep in Pittsburgh.

With their accomplished new drummer, Rush hit the road for three months in the crucible. A handful of American dates in August '74 led

into a home stand in late October. Through November and December, the band found their home in America's rustbelt, also hitting parts of the eastern and western US. The most memorable of headliners were Kiss, although Rush also shared stages with Eastwind, Rory Gallagher, Law, Don Preston, Rainbow Canyon, Rare Earth, Sha Na Na, Sweetleaf, Uriah Heep.

"I think we spent more time in the north," remembers Alex, trying to map that first tour in his mind. "Those first shows were Cleveland, Pittsburgh, Jonestown, Pennsylvania, and we did other gigs spread out among those big tours we were doing, all in really small venues, opening for other bands. I don't think we headed south until later in the year, after a couple of months of touring. We also did a lot of dates with Rory Gallagher in that first swing, and that was great. I was a fan of his then, and he was such a gracious guy, all just really, really nice people. And I got to watch him every night; that was the best."

The sets opened stealth-like with the surging riff of Finding My Way gathering steam. Second selection was Best I Can, which wouldn't make it to record until **Fly by Night**. Anthem from that record was also an early live tune. From **Rush**, only Before and After was not part of the set list. Finally, headlining or not, the band found time and space for Peart's drum solo, housed within the heaving critical mass of Working Man.

Alex recalls those days, specifically addressing the topic of first meeting any of his own musical heroes. "We opened four shows; Uriah Heep was headlining, and it was all arenas, Manfred Mann and us as backup. We'd gone from those few hundred people in a club to 12, 13,000 people, doing a 20-minute set with a stage the size of this table. You know, there was no room, three acts. That was so nerve-wracking but so exciting at the same time. I think we played three songs. Working Man was over ten minutes and then a couple of other shorter songs, and that was it.

"And I remember meeting Ken Hensley and Mick Box from Uriah Heep, and they were great, especially Ken, just the sweetest guy, a really, really nice guy. He signed a bunch of pictures for me, for friends, and gave fatherly advice, all this kind of stuff. And it was really nice meeting somebody like that. You have your preconceived ideas of how people are, and they were just very genuine and helpful. And years later they opened for us, after being out of the scene and trying to get back together. And, boy, we went out of our way to make sure that they got everything, a soundcheck and everything in their rider, a couple of bottles of champagne from us . . . all that stuff.

"There was one gig," laughs Alex, warming to the topic of old war stories. "I think it was in Decatur, Illinois, and we got there, and it was a

club gig. We got there a little bit early — the truck was maybe 20 minutes behind us — and we walked in, and it was a tiny club with a stage maybe about eight feet deep and about 30 feet long. And there was no way we could get our gear on there, let alone play. And we went to the owner and said 'Hi, we're Rush, and we have a problem here. We can't get our equipment on the stage.' And he said, 'Why not, isn't it just an acoustic guitar and some chairs?' And we said, 'No, it's drums and amps,' and he said, 'Well, wait a second . . . Tom Rush?! Isn't that Tom Rush?' 'No, this is Rush.' So obviously the gig was canceled. But he paid us anyway."

Neil adds his recollections of those early days on the road. "Well, when I first toured in '74, one of the earliest ones was opening for Sha Na Na at a Baltimore high school. And it was my 22nd birthday. They didn't like us [laughs]. That was one of the worst matchups in history, until, five years later, let's say, when Blondie opened for us [laughs]. Bad choice [Blondie, booed off the stage, was a last-minute replacement at a Philadelphia stop on the **Hemispheres** tour.) There were those kinds of mismarriages."

Geddy, on the same subject, adds, "Eclectic live billings? Yeah, I've got a few. How about Rush, Billy Preston and Kiss? That's pretty eclectic. And we did a festival in Holland once where it was The Police, ourselves and Peter Tosh [Pink Pop Festival, June 4th, 1979 — Mick Jagger and Dire Straits were also part of this bill; Alex soldiered on despite a broken finger]. I believe we played with Motörhead. I know I played with Lemmy on a couple of occasions; it might have been with Hawkwind, but they weren't really heavy; they were fun and stoned. There was a time when they all seemed to be heavy, thrash metal bands, and then there was this big-hair metal period where all the opening acts seemed to blend into one. . . ."

"In 30 years of touring, anything that could happen happened," muses Neil. "One of the early shows too was a club in San Antonio, and the promoter was arguing with our tour manager about the fee and all that stuff, and at one point he just put a gun on the table.

"Our career spans the '70s, the '80s, the '90s, and a lot was going on in the world in those times. That's what I realize about writing about being a young musician. It's not just about my life but about my life and times, you know, growing up through the '60s and '70s, being a young musician in the '60s and '70s. A lot of stuff was going around it all. You could call that the frame, but necessarily it had an osmotic effect on the music and the music of the times."

Fly by Night

Recorded in January of '75, and released the following month, *Fly by Night* would be the first album for the Rush lineup as it exists today and a quantum leap ahead of the blue-collar, barroom rock postures of the debut. Wintery and dramatic from the cover art right on down through the somehow Canuck-souled songs, *Fly by Night* would forever retain a respectable reputation  through the progressive pop of the title track, through the convoluted crunch of *Anthem* (in reference to the Ayn Rand book of the same title) and *Beneath, Between and Behind* and, most prominently, through the brisk, slashing, progressive metal blueprinting of *By-Tor and the Snow Dog*. Heck, even golden oldie *Best I Can* gets an unexpected bounce from that new drummer there. Put this song on *Rush* and it's nowhere near as . . . sparkly. The album draws to a close with two light, somewhat forgotten numbers in *Making Memories* and *Rivendell* (neither was part of the ensuing tour's set list, the only compositions, in fact, that weren't), even the final track *In the End* starting plush and barely audible before transforming into languid, melodic, hard rock worthy of fireside sipping while the giant snowy owl outside menaces.

On March 24th, 1975, Rush would also wind up with their first of many Juno awards, winning what is jokingly considered a curse, the title for Most Promising Group. Two weeks before that, Alex had married Charlene, girlfriend since the late '60s, already the mother of their first child, Justin.

"**Fly by Night** was a very busy time," explains Alex. "We had just finished the first leg of an American tour. We had been on the road from August of '74 up until Christmas. We went into the studio to record **Fly by Night**, and it was done in about five days, if I remember correctly. We went in one morning and recorded the record, through the five-day period, finished mixing it about three or four o'clock in the morning and packed up and went directly to the airport for an 8:00 a.m. flight to do a gig in Winnipeg. That was murder. We got to Winnipeg, and it was so cold. So we basically had no time off. We finished the date, came home, went into the studio and left from the studio to go back on the road. But great memories of it as well; it was a very exciting time. The ball was just beginning to roll for us.

"*Best I Can* is an earlier song from the old days," continues Alex, perusing the back album cover. "*Making Memories*, I remember, that was written on a drive where we got lost. It was in the Midwest somewhere, Indiana maybe. I forget where we were going to, but we made a right, and we should've made a left [laughs]. We went out of our way by a few hours, and we were sitting in the car with an acoustic guitar, and that's the way we wrote songs then. Pretty much everything was written in dressing rooms and soundchecks. Neil's lyrics were written on the road. That one was all written before we went into the studio."

I posed the same question to Neil that I had asked Alex, whether the band had any awareness that all of a sudden they were the only band combining progressive rock and heavy metal — until a decade later, in fact, with the rise of Queensryche, Fates Warning and eventually Dream

Theater (one may posit that Deep Purple, Led Zeppelin and Uriah Heep also played in the same soundbox, although not to the fingers flyin' extent of Rush).

"Yeah," laughs Peart, more so at being called a grandfather of progressive metal. "I noticed that with the rap and rock combination. I thought that Faith No More were so amazing when they first came out, and then there was Cypress Hill and Rage Against the Machine, and then it just kind of bubbles along for a while until it suddenly exploded. And reggae and rock was like that too. Reggae bubbled along beneath the radar, and then suddenly in the late '70s — boom.

"But we just played what we liked. We were always that organic, and still are, all through those changes. It was just about trying to play the music we liked. I've made the quote before, 'I loved music so much, I wanted to play it.' That's the fundamental chemical reaction that went on. At that time, we had a foot in both camps, stylistically, as young musicians. We'd grown up with The Who, Led Zeppelin, Yardbirds and the birth of hard rock. And at the same time, we were fans of the whole progressive scene. So for us, it was just an expression of what we liked. There was no 'Let's synthesize these two styles; if we take that element and combine it with this element, we'll have something new!' It was nothing like that. We were never that self-aware, let alone that calculating. It was simply an organic response to playing what we liked. We liked to play loud and energetically, and this new complicated, sophisticated approach appealed as well."

"We were influenced by bands like Yes, Genesis, Van Der Graaf Generator, Gentle Giant and ELP," adds Geddy on the same subject. "They were progressive bands in every sense of the word, and as musicians we were influenced by that kind of playing and structure. So the fact that we were born out of a love for rock and metal — whatever you want to call it — I mean, that's how we started, admiring bands like Cream and The Who. And when the progressive movement came along,

we were so impressed with the musicality and the complexity, we became complexity freaks. So we wanted to write things that were heavy but complex."

And then the arrival of Peart, Geddy explains, sealed the deal. "It has to do more with the period than anything. Alex and I were already starting to write more complex stuff, and part of what wasn't working with our first drummer was the fact that he was more of a rock purist, and Alex and I wanted to play more complex stuff. And Neil coming into the band was a kind of confirming final piece of the puzzle. That was very much where he was at. He liked to play things that were very difficult to play, and that was the direction Alex and I were moving in. It had a very catalytic effect."

The **Fly by Night** tour kicked off with a home stand in February of '75, and then it was directly into the US south, plus all the various middles and points west, closing off with a considerably detailed trek through Ontario. February and March were light, but April, May and June were full-on nonstop. Rush shared the spotlight with such luminaries as James Gang, The Kidds, Steve Long Group, Sky King, Sweetleaf, Symphonic Slam, The Tubes and Vitale's Madmen. But the majority of the dates found the band opening for Kiss.

"Oh, we did a million shows with Kiss," says Alex, clarifying the exact number. "In '75, we were playing on average 3,000-seaters, so small theaters. We weren't big bands at all. This was for both of us our first tours. And we became quite close, very good friends; we hung out all the time. Days off we got together, went out for dinner. On show days, we were always in each other's dressing rooms. We corresponded when we were off the road. We really became quite close, and really, I think, it was because we were sharing this whole new experience.

"We would sit down and talk to Paul and Gene about music, where we were coming from, where they were coming from. And it was interesting to hear them talk about what Kiss represented; they knew what kind of music they needed to make for this thing to work. And I remember both of them sitting in my hotel room one night. I think it was in Louisville, Kentucky, with two acoustics, and they were singing all these other songs, and they were really nice songs that they'd written that would never be Kiss songs! And, of course, we were from a whole different area, where it wasn't about the showbiz. It was all about the music and playing.

"And we just sort of lost touch with them when the live album came out and they became huge, although we did go out to see them a couple times. Ace was a riot. Ace was very, very funny. And he loved getting messed up. He loved drinking and smoking pot, anything to get messed up. But he always had some new joke to tell you. For his birthday, we got him a couple of gifts, just little goofy things, and invited him down to one of our rooms. We were sharing rooms then too. And we got a bunch of booze and smoked some pot and celebrated his birthday with him, and he said [impersonating Ace's high voice], 'You know, you guys . . . I can't believe it. The band members in the band I play in don't even wish me happy birthday, and you get me all these gifts, and you get me down here. Like, you guys are the best! You're the best!' I remember asking him — he got a new house — and I said, 'How's your new house, Ace?' [impersonating Ace again] 'I find it very accommodating. Yuk yuk yuk yuk.' He was really a lot of fun. And Peter was a nice guy too."

The tour for **Fly by Night**'s follow-up, **Caress of Steel**, would be the last Rush would do with Kiss. "By then, we were getting to the point where we were probably a little too big to tour for them," says Alex. "They were looking for something smaller as an opening act and maybe something that was a little more in line with what they were doing."

Geddy cites Kiss when asked for examples of excess he saw on tour. "Traveling with Kiss before they started to get successful. . . . Kiss were always very frustrated because they would walk offstage, take off their makeup, and nobody would know it was them. So it was very hard for them to get recognized, and they didn't like that. So they would have these wild parties after the show and invite, you know, everyone in sight. So there was some pretty serious goings-on. But we were good friends. We toured together for the first two tours of America for us, and we had a very good relationship. They were not successful yet, so we were playing small theaters together. We didn't have any trouble at all."

On June 7th, 1975, in San Diego, before returning home for some closing Canadian dates, Rush received a memorable send-off from Gene, Paul, Ace and Peter. "We had a big whipped cream scene at the end of our tour with them," admits Alex. "They just creamed us with cream pies; it was serious. I was getting stuff out of my guitar pickups for weeks afterwards." At the end of the Kiss set, Rush got their revenge, resulting in a stage covered in shaving cream and a turgid encore from the rapidly ascending headliners.

San Diego, along with a sold-out April '75 support date to 4,500 at the Michigan Palace in Detroit (home away from home for Kiss; Rush's might be Cleveland!), would prove to be memorable touring highlights for years to come. A headlining gig at Massey Hall, Max Webster in tow, would also prove to be a landmark, not to mention a warm-up for the shows that would become the band's first live album a year and a half later, with, shockingly, two studio albums in the interim.

"We toured a lot with Aerosmith that year too," continues Alex, fortunate or unfortunate to run into another juggernaut near off the rails. "The Aerosmith tours were not the most satisfying for us. We didn't get one single soundcheck in, I don't know how many dates we did, 50 dates. I remember one time Neil changed the skins on his drums, and he needed to tune his drums backstage. He was doing it there because we didn't have a soundcheck. And the crew guys came up and said, 'Shut the fuck up!!' You know, he couldn't even tune his drums. He had to move his drums into the dressing room to tune them. They were just really . . . we just stayed out of their way as much as we could.

"Years later Howard Ungerleider, our lighting designer, was on a flight to Europe, and they were on the plane, and Steven came over. This was after they fell apart and went through their dark period and reformed and came back to life. He came up and sat with Howard and said, 'You know, I just have bad memories of the way we treated people back then. You know, tell the guys we're really sorry about that, and maybe one day we can get together and just have a chat.' So I thought

that was pretty cool of him to have remembered that and made that effort.

"And, you know, you learn from those sorts of things. We always went out of our way to make sure that any opening act that played with us got a soundcheck and got everything they required in their rider. We really bent over backwards for everyone. It was really because of those sorts of experiences where you didn't get stuff. It just didn't seem right. It's just such a great experience and so much fun, and every touring band shares in that. You should be brothers. You shouldn't try to put each other off. Some people look at it as a very competitive thing. 'Gotta blow 'em off the stage tonight!' You do your own thing; that's it."

Neil gets the final word on the subject, remarking with a chuckle, "Aerosmith were one of the bands that was a good example of what not to do!"

Caress
of Steel

Rush's third album, Caress of Steel, alas, is considered many things, none of them too flattering. It is the band's black hole, conversely a bit of a snicker, too much too soon, the epitome of prog rock excess, a record pumped and primed for bad reviews, of which Alex was all too keenly aware. "Most of the comments back then were 'energized rock,' 'Geddy's high shrieking voice,' 'very Led Zeppelin knockoffish,' that sort of thing. Mostly we didn't get good reviews. In fact, I don't really remember having a lot of good reviews for a long time. We would get good press in magazines like Circus, for example, but Creem hated us, because they thought we were pretentious, we were too serious, and that's not what rock 'n' roll is all about. And a lot of the New York press was like that. I mean, the bad press we used to get was really, really bad. They went out of their way to just take shots at us. And after a while, it didn't really faze us; we didn't care. We were doing what we were doing, and we were starting to develop our own audience that cared about the music, and that's all that counted. And here we are 30 years later celebrating our 30th anniversary, and none of those journalists are around anymore."

Caress of Steel is, however, a logical, even brave, follow-up to **Fly by Night** in that it takes that record's more progressive moments and builds a (nearly) cohesive whole out of them. And both the band's ambition and their subsequent meticulousness make for an album that is not embarrassing, one with regularly recurring fresh ideas, not to mention trio-mad chemistry topped with a shriek to behold. Indeed, two of the album's tracks are considered classics, no irony or wink or nudge needed. *Bastille Day* is a barnstormer of a speed metaller, one of the band's heaviest three or four songs, wrapped around a tale of the French Revolution, vocals on fire. *Lakeside Park* (although, really, the band is none too fond of it) is a nice nostalgic popster nestled lovingly between *Fly by Night* and *Closer to the Heart*. Memorializing Neil's dream teen summer job down at the fair in Port Dalhousie, Ontario, the track has stubbornly stuck around as a minor radio staple.

Then there's the curious case of *I Think I'm Going Bald*, a boogie rocker similar to *In the Mood* and a host of blues-derived hard rock hits and also-rans from years such as 1972. "We were touring a lot with Kiss in those days," says Geddy, "and they had a song called *I Think I'm Going Blind* [actually just *Goin' Blind*]. So we were kind of taking the piss out of that title by just coming up with this. . . . Pratt [a nickname for Neil, another one being The Professor] came up with this line, 'I think I'm going bald,'

because Alex is always worried about losing his hair. Even when he was not losing his hair, he was obsessed with the fact that he might lose his hair. So he would try all kinds of ingredients to put on his scalp. And I think it just got Neil thinking about aging, even though we weren't aging yet and had no right to talk about that stuff yet. It would be much more appropriate now. And it just became a kind of funny song. And even though the song is not funny, in terms of the sentiment, it kind of is, and the music is really goofy. A lot of people mistake us for being deadly serious, but some of our songs are just plain goofy."

Then the record wings out, offering 12 and a half minutes of Tolkien-styled fantasy with *The Necromancer*, a creepy, quite heavy, often jarring prog metal opus, and 20 minutes of *The Fountain of Lamneth*, a more meandering, Floydian, Zep-like, melodic and thus less malevolent prog monster that cycles through a man's life and achievement-steeped tribulations from birth to death.

"*Fountain of Lamneth* was just something we had to do," notes Geddy with a laugh. "But it's kind of absurd. I mean, it's just where we were at. We were a young band, a little pretentious, full of ambitions, full of grand ideas, and we wanted to see if we could make some of those grand ideas happen. And *Fountain of Lamneth* was the first attempt at that. And I think there are some beautiful moments, but a lot of it is ponderous and

off the mark. A lot of that album is for that reason. It's also the most time we ever had to make a record. I think we had a full three weeks to make that record [laughs]. And we were just languishing, indulging ourselves, oodles of time. You know, **Fly by Night** was made in ten days. Now we had three weeks, and there were a lot of funny aromas in the control room too [laughs]."

The dark, alchemical (lead-poisoned?) cover art for **Caress of Steel** would be fashioned by Hugh Syme, then keyboardist for Moon Records act Ian Thomas. Fancying a go, Hugh would, in fact, work with the band on every subsequent album. Other signature pieces would be designed for the likes of Megadeth, Queensryche, Fates Warning, Kim Mitchell, Whitesnake, Coverdale Page and Aerosmith.

Back into the sounds, Alex sums up **Caress of Steel** this way. "That was a very experimental album for us. On **Fly by Night**, we had By-Tor. By-Tor was that first experimental song where we stretched out a little bit. It had a lot of parts to it and was a long song, almost nine minutes. So that was really the precursor to this; *Necromancer* was an extension of

By-Tor. But *The Fountain of Lamneth* became even more of that experimental, full-side, thematic . . . I don't want to say opera, but concept kind of record. I mean, we were experimenting then, to see what would work. And that was very challenging. It was really important for us to do that. The record company, I think, hated it. It was the least commercially successful record that we've done."

Unquestionably still a backup band at this point, Rush clutched a set list that was none too long. Yet all of the short snappers from the album, plus *The Necromancer*, made the grade. Back home at Massey Hall on January 10th, 1976, to close the tour, the band even trotted out *The Fountain of Lamneth*. Only two demoralizing months long, the **Caress of Steel** tour (soon dubbed The Down the Tubes Tour) was on the back of an album floundering, reversing the modest upward trajectory of its hopeful, politely intrusive predecessors. Indeed, **Fly by Night** had gone gold in Canada. So, back to reality, Rush was out there, supporting Kiss again, supporting Ted Nugent, doing isolated shows with Lynyrd Skynyrd, Mott (no Hoople), Leslie West, Artful Dodger and Mendelson Joe.

"We did have some really good times with Mott," recalls Alex fondly of his **Caress of Steel** tourmates. "They were sort of on the back end of their career; Ian Hunter wasn't in the band at the time. They were just trying to make a last stab. We got along really well with them and had some really fun times. Ted Nugent, we did a lot of shows with Ted, all over the country, mostly smaller sorts of arenas or secondary markets. He was such an interesting guy, but he was crazy at a time when crazy meant drinking, that sort of crazy. He was nuts, but he was super straight and very conservative. Even though he had really long hair, he had really conservative ideas about things. But he was always full of energy, and he was great to us. We hung out with Ted. We were special guesting, and somebody else was opening. We always got our soundchecks, we always got our encores, never a problem."

It is of interest that Neil can barely be drawn into any detailed analysis of records such as **Fly by Night** and **Caress of Steel**. When asked to compare the two, or perhaps cite the band's advancement between the two, he offers a good-natured "No. Oh, those were the growing years, and I often equate that to

RUSH
IN CONCERT
SPECIAL GUEST ARTISTS
JOE MENDELSON AND TRIONE
Saturday, June 21st, 1975
8:30 p.m.
MEMORIAL GARDENS

No. 865

ADVANCE TICKETS — — $3.50

children's drawings on the refrigerator that hang around too long, you know [laughs]? I really wish that they would just go away. I think we really started . . . wow, given my druthers, I would make our first album **Moving Pictures**. I can't think of a single reason not to do that!

"It's, like, even with book writing. I wrote probably ten books before I published one. And I'm really glad to have had that luxury, doing all my experimenting and getting it all out of my system, doing my stream-of-consciousness writing and doing my six-adjectives-per-noun writing, getting that out of my system privately! And then by the time I was ready to publish, I had a book that I can still live with years later.

"And music, unfortunately, isn't like that. You do your growing up in public, and it's there forever. I still turn on the radio, and there's a song that makes me cringe. But that's the reality of it. In answer to your question, a lot of it I have a personal affection for — **Hemispheres** and all that — just for the time it represented and what we were doing and the men we were and the people we were. But I don't necessarily think it ever needs to be heard again."

2112

2112 would prove to be the album — with Kiss it was Alive! — that would save the band's listing career. Punchier but nearly as conceptual as Caress of Steel, 2112 would benefit from a thicker, warmer sound, an effect that really drove home the increased levels of power chording. In fact, A Passage to Bangkok, Something for Nothing and The Temples of Syrinx would rank as the band's heaviest compositions ever. In other Federation news, Alex would pen the lyrics to the pert, poppy, then crunching (and vaguely BTO-ish) Lessons, while Geddy would wordsmith a haunting, ambitiously arranged ballad called Tears.

However, the centerpiece of the album is undoubtedly the side-long title track. A tale about a future in which music is banned after being deemed superfluous and against logic, 2112 is more about oppression, questions of freedoms and how many we should have, an area of study near and dear to Peart's heart, given his Ayn Rand readings at the time. The crowning graphic image for both the record and the tour would be the lurid red pentagram ("If someone gets something else out of that, you know, that's their problem," laughs Alex), which became an enduring Rush symbol. For Peart, the sign had nothing to do with Satan, representing instead the creativity-suffocating authorities of the tension-filled tale. Prerelease, Geddy spoke of the song as being a science fiction tale concerned with individuality and how society's leadership — consisting of computers and priests — prefers that everybody be programmed to be homogeneous.

"2112 is probably the most important thing we've ever written," says Geddy firmly. "Because without that song, we probably would not have continued as a band. It was largely written in studio and in rehearsal, and I think we had four weeks to make that record, so we got an extra week out of the deal, from **Caress of Steel** [laughs]. And it just came together. Even some of the heaviest parts Alex and I wrote just sitting down together with acoustic guitars. The concept came together very clearly, very quickly. We just had these riffs we wanted to put together, and it just started to click for that song. And that whole album is very much like that.

"Alex had a turn of writing on his own, and we just wanted to throw everything into the mix. My memory of it is that we were all very much in the same direction. Whenever we talked about what a song should be . . . 'Yeah, that's right!' We knew right away. There wasn't a lot of second-guessing; there wasn't a lot of 'Should we treat it like this? Should we treat it like that?' We all knew how we wanted to play that song and write that song. And we had really just dug the concept Neil had come up with."

"**2112** was written on the road just before we recorded it," explains Alex, referring to the album, not the song. "And, you know, that came from a different place, more from a place of defiance and anger that things were sort of going the way they were around us. So we were fighting back. That was quite a spontaneous record. Obviously, there was

planning and work done beforehand. We went into the studio armed with all the material.

"There was a lot of pressure from us, from the record company and, to some degree, from management to go back to our rock roots, make another **Rush** album. And we basically said, 'You know what? That's not what we're about. If that's what everybody wants, then that's what they're not going to get. If we go down, we're going to go down in flames.' And I remember having this discussion in our van. We were so despondent. We thought we were doing what was right and learning and that this was a stepping stone. But there was no support, anywhere, for us.

"So we were pissed off. So we thought, 'You know what? We're just going to do what we do.' And we started writing **2112**. And there's a lot of passion and anger on that record. And we couldn't have done that without **Caress of Steel** and feeling kind of alone. And **2112** turned out to be our ticket to independence. After that, the record company said, 'Fine, do whatever you want. You guys have proved that you know what you're doing, for you.' So there's never been anybody from the record company in any of our sessions ever. Ray's never been at any of our sessions. It's always a closed-door thing. We write the music, play it, whatever we feel is right, and it's up to them to work with that. But I don't think we could have accomplished any of that without cutting our teeth on **Caress of Steel**, which was a very important record for us creatively."

Digging a bit more into the logistics of the album, Alex recalls that the band "didn't have a lot of time to record; we were always touring. So most of our material was written on the road. Very little of it was left to the studio. At least we had very clear sketches of what we wanted to do. **2112** was recorded in about a week and a half, something like that. You know [laughs], quite a difference from an album like **Vapor Trails**, which took 14 months. But we were prepared; everything was really direct, we plugged in. I think it was all eight track at that time, so you didn't have a lot of room to do overdubs and get all crazy; it was very, very straightforward.

"So, yeah, everybody had invested a lot of time and money in us, and there was a real concern that it wasn't going to work out. And we had decided, we can either make another Rush album like the first album, or we're just going to stick to our guns and do what we think is right for us. I think we all felt very strongly that that was the kind of writing we wanted to do and that we felt that was unique to us, and that's what we wanted to pursue. We were into that mode of wanting to write a more conceptual piece for the whole record. So with the backing of *Fountain of Lamneth* from **Caress of Steel**, which was our foray into writing in that mode, that's really what 2112 came out of. And, like I say, that really bought us our independence from everybody. After that, everybody left us alone to do what we thought was right."

Rush's **2112** tour, which blends into the **All the World's a Stage** tour, was a 15-month odyssey that stretched from early March '76 to June '77. March and April found the band chewing up the American West Coast plus making some eastern and central Canadian dates. May and July covered the American Midwest and the South respectively. In June of '76, the band set up for three hometown dates at Massey Hall (the third added due to demand) to record their seminal first live album. In September, the band continued their grueling attack on the States, starting in the Northeast, with a side trip back home for nine Canadian dates. Back in the US, the band began in the West, hopped back home for three Canadian dates around the new year, then covered Texas, the Midwest, two dates in California, then back to the band's bread and butter, the Midwest, the east and the dependable rustbelt. June of '77 marked the first time Rush would tour Europe (an early tour had been canceled), the band landing in England for seven dates, with a single show logged in Stockholm, Sweden, a country Geddy had said in the press was the band's second best market with respect to record sales.

Given the jumble of headline and support slots as the band made their move up the ladder (of note, the band would not do well in the

northeastern US for years), the set lists for the massive **2112** tour varied greatly. With respect to the new album, however, a truncated version of the title opus made the grade (mainly less the angular *Oracle: The Dream*), as did *The Twilight Zone* and fiery speed rocker *Something for Nothing*. Interestingly, *A Passage to Bangkok* (lyrically, a brief, amusing travel journal citing world drug destinations) would not be added until the **Hemispheres** campaign.

As usual, Rush found themselves billed with a bewildering cavalcade of bands on their way up, on their way down or on their way sideways. Rush provided support for Aerosmith, Blue Öyster Cult, Boston, Kansas, Lynyrd Skynyrd, Ted Nugent, REO Speedwagon, Styx, Thin Lizzy, while lording elegantly over Angel, Artful Dodger, Be-Bop Deluxe, Tommy Bolin, Cheap Trick, Chilliwack, Stu Daye, Derringer, Fat Tuesday, Head East, Max Webster, Rex, Roller, The Runaways, Smokehouse, Starcastle, Stray, Sutherland Brothers Quiver, T. Rex and Wireless, also, like Rush, an Anthem act, whose '80 **No Static** album Geddy would produce.

Alex says with an implied wink that both Neil and Geddy were entirely complicit in the drinking and partying camaraderie found between a rising Rush and the bands with which they shared the grinding rise to

prominence. "Oh, totally. Absolutely! You know, we were a lot younger then. That was a long time ago — 25 years ago. It was the same thing with the Thin Lizzy guys. We got so tight with them; I love those guys. They were great. Brian Robertson and I . . . you know, we became really close friends, and we hung out all the time. Talk about drinking . . . it was not unusual to drink almost a bottle of Scotch a night, just because you were fired up and that's the way it was. And they were coming from the same sort of place we were musically. They cared a lot about their music."

Blue Öyster Cult was also at the same place on the career ladder, having broken out finally right around the time of a double live album. "They were really good to us and were really nice guys," notes Alex. "We got along really well with them, no problems with us that I can recall. I really respected Buck [Dharma, real name Donald Roeser] a lot. We spent time together, and we did a lot of dates with them. The crews got along really, really well. And we opened for them, I think, through that whole time. They opened for us for a series of shows in the Midwest, '84-ish. My God, I can't believe that it was over 20 years ago that we did those shows.

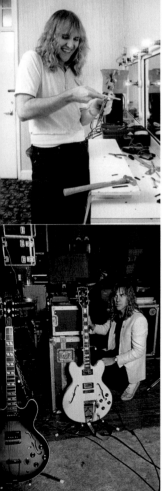

"One thing [laughs], they have a song called *Godzilla* that started off with that stomping [makes big footstep sounds], and the tape of Godzilla coming, and they do the whole rap before it: 'As he rounded the corner and he looked down. . . .' And we substituted their tape where he roars, or whatever, with a tape of Mr. Ed. 'And he said . . . "Hello, my name is Mr. Ed,"' and they all stopped on stage with their mouths open, speechless, stuttering . . . [laughs].

"We did some shows with Bob Seger that were mostly Midwestern shows," continues Alex. "I remember one night — I can't remember if it was Flint or Saginaw or someplace like that — and we got an encore and came out and played the song, and we left the stage, and people were still going mental. And the band were on the side of the stage going 'Come on! Come on!' to get us back on and do another encore. I mean, that never happens! House lights [snaps his finger] usually go on immediately. But they were so cool, those guys. I remember them as being probably the nicest people we ever worked with. They were all such gentlemen, really, really good people."

Geddy figures that **2112** marked the germination of the monster cinematic presentations that would increasingly accompany Rush's music live on stage. "In our history, I think we went through every kind of possible projection system that anyone's ever used, from the early days when we actually had almost like a Grateful Dead-like system using oil and colors, things like that, which originate from our very, very first tours when we used lights. There was a guy, Tim, out of Virginia, who used to work with our sound company, National Sound; he would bring out some extra lights. This is when we were just starting to headline, a couple of gigs here, a couple of gigs there. It must have been early **2112**. And then we wanted to project the **2112** logo on the back of the screen. And I think that's how we started getting into this whole visual thing, this whole filmic thing, just with those few ideas. We actually, I think, used a little projector, like one of those ones you used to use in school [laughs]."

At the time, Geddy remarked that the band had recently considered an expansion but had decided after a vote to learn more instruments themselves, in addition to experimenting with slide shows for the live presentations. As elucidation, Geddy mentions 16-string and 12-string guitars, double necks, bass pedal synthesizer, vibes and orchestra bells (Neil said at the time that the bass pedals were for *Lakeside Park*). Geddy also lamented the fact that Canada Customs made it difficult for the band to bring their full light show (projectors, etc.) north of the border.

"I was so impressed, in Britain, with the audience and how they listened," notes Alex, adding his impressions of that first minitour overseas. "During a song, they would just stand there, or sit, and listen, and then at the end of the song 'rooaaarrr,' and then the next song. Very seldom did you hear anybody yell during a song, unless it's one of those big stops

where the whole crowd kind of cheers. That's really what impressed me with all of Europe, really. In Holland, it was the same thing, the way people responded to certain parts of certain songs. They have a whole different appreciation. When you talk to people about music, they can be fans of Abba, or some heavy metal, Black Sabbath, to use an early example. They were so diverse in their musical interests. And that really, really impressed me. And they're more of a polite audience to play to. Whereas in America, especially if you're playing the Detroit area, there's stuff whipping around, and people are going mental all the time."

Which leads to the inevitable subject of onstage injuries. What's the tally? Alex answers, "I think Geddy got hit with a bolt once, a bottle once, a bullet, like the shell case and the whole thing. I was hit with the glow-sticks. In terms of real injuries, actually Geddy got hit one time pretty hard with a bottle. I think it glanced him, and I think it cut his forehead or something. We had to stop the show for a few minutes. I don't think Neil was ever hurt."

How about pyro disasters or quickly unhinging lighting rigs? "No, thank God," Alex continues. "Is there some wood around here to knock on? Not really, no. There was a PA horn that fell off the stage at Nassau Coliseum. We were playing with Blue Öyster Cult, in fact. And it had fallen back off the stage-right stack, onto the stage, fell back and decapitated my double neck, sheared the head stock off the double neck, and it fell over on an old Gibson that I had on the road with me that I retired after that. It was just too valuable to me to have on the road."

Alex then takes stock of the travel arrangements up to the point of this first properly successful album and tour and beyond. "That's actually interesting. We were in rental cars, well, a rental sedan [casualties, through '75 and 11,000 miles, included the mirror, radio and all the hubcaps], for the first year, and then we were in a station wagon for I guess the following year.

"And then we got a van, maybe around the time of **2112**. It was a Funcraft van, a Dodge van with a cap on it and a back seating area you could fold down into a bed. It had a table and two bench seats and this little area over the driver that you could climb up and sleep in. And there were five of us in there, I guess? And we took shifts driving. We all took 350-mile shifts, and it was smelly [laughs] and a mess, but it was sure a lot of fun. We had that thing for a couple of years. We went through, I think, three motors in it, and we traveled, boy, 100 and something thousand miles in the time that we had that in those couple of years.

"And then we graduated to a Barth motor home. I mean, it was the ugliest thing you've ever seen. It was a big shoebox on wheels. It figures

that we would pick something like that [laughs] instead of one of those more elegant Winnebagos or those other ones that were more stream-lined, Gulfstream or whatever it's called.

"And we had that for a couple of years, and then finally we got a bus, I think around the time of **A Farewell to Kings** or **Hemispheres**. You know, we just couldn't afford it. But there weren't many buses around at that time. And when you get in a bus now . . . boy, it would've been nice to have one done up like that back then."

But success was beginning to show rewards. "It was probably about the time of **2112**. We got more booze in the dressing room. We went from those couple of bottles of Blue Nun, to having a bottle of Scotch one night, to having a bottle of Courvoisier the next night. The food got better. It wasn't just the deli tray with the local white bread."

All the World's a Stage

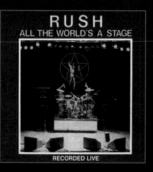

RUSH
ALL THE WORLD'S A STAGE

RECORDED LIVE

The double live album with triple gatefold that was All the World's a Stage came at a time when folks such as Kiss, Blue Öyster Cult, Peter Frampton — and later Ted Nugent, Aerosmith and Judas Priest — found considerable success with the format. Mercury wanted a live album, and the band was only too happy to comply. In fact, Rush wanted a live album out after three albums, which pointedly worked wonders for Kiss, who had been floundering with Dressed to Kill (as Rush was with Caress of Steel) before blowing up big with Alive!.

As mentioned, Rush set up at the venerable and plush Massey Hall in hometown Toronto, midway through the **2112** tour, for the premeditated recording. "We brought the truck in and had a very in-depth sound-check," recalls Alex. "I think we might have even set up the day before and did a good, solid soundcheck. And I just remember how nerve-wracking that was. Playing your hometown is always nerve-wracking [laughs], always crazy. Knowing that the truck was out there and the record button was on, you were so nervous and so afraid of making mistakes and clunkers and things like that. I don't think we did anything," says Alex with respect to touch-ups. "That's such a long time ago. We might have done a couple of vocal things, maybe? But even that doesn't sound familiar to me." The record, however, did go through three remixes.

"The first live album was very raw; it was the first time we ever recorded the band live, over three days," says Geddy. "We basically took the best of what we had, which to some fans is very exciting, and from our point of view it's a little difficult to listen to, because it sounds a little crude. But that's the nature of that album. In terms of the work on it, I think we were all pretty involved, us and Terry Brown, because I think he coproduced it with us.

"Probably the funniest thing to do with that album was the way we ended it. We had this long applause, and in the end we faded the applause into this sound of Alex, Neil and myself in the parking lot clapping our hands. We put it long into the thing, so you really have to let the applause

run to the end of the groove to hear it. The applause fades into the three of us in the parking lot clapping, and then we say, 'Okay, see you later,' and then we get into a car, and you hear the car door slam, and then we drive away."

As alluded to, this juggernaut of an album sort of co-opted the **2112** tour, the critical mass of both albums keeping the band on the road for what would be their longest more or less uninterrupted stretch ever, contributing to a bad case of road burn that would find its nadir with the **A Farewell to Kings** tour all too close around the next corner. A live single featuring *Fly by Night*, *In the Mood* and *Something for Nothing* helped to fuel the fire and keep the band's heads and wheels spinning. And, indeed, proving the premise that the mid-'70s was indeed the golden years for live records, **All the World's a Stage** actually charted higher in the States than **2112**, beating out the studio album by a score of #40 to #61 (and far outdistancing **Caress of Steel** at #148).

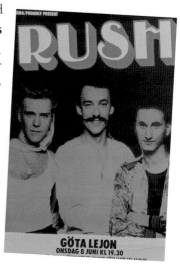

In the world of personal news, a month after the Massey Hall stand, Geddy married Nancy, who was actually the sister of early Rush alumnus Lindy Young.

A Farewell
to Kings

All the World's a Stage contained a liner message calling the record "the close of chapter one." And, indeed,
A Farewell to Kings (working title Closer to the
Heart) fulfills the promise of a new chapter begun,
Rush writing and arranging much more exotically
than ever before, less often looking into the eye of the
heavy metal storm, only arriving at that place when
the new songs — occasionally, rarely, deliberately —
require that particularly exaggerated electricity as
nourishment.

And nourishing the new record was. The listener
felt the band's enthusiasm, a mutual replenishment
taking place, a buoyancy shared, flights of fancy booked
at a group discount. If the following sounds a bit like
Pagey talking about Zeppelin III, well . . . go ahead and
compare the two records.

"It really wasn't until **Kings** that we went somewhere and had dedicated writing time," says Alex wistfully. "And the interesting thing is, we were writing on an acoustic guitar, Geddy and I. I think all the stuff was written on an acoustic guitar — although they were rock songs — with no kind of recording situation until we could get a boombox later and kind of throw our ideas onto that."

"All those songs were recorded at Rockfield in Wales, and recording there was really an experience," adds Geddy, who tantalizingly had hinted before the release of the album that Rush would be pursuing a direction somewhat akin to Yes meets Led Zeppelin. "It was the first time we had worked away from home at a residential studio. Here we are in Wales, and the sun never shines in Wales, for weeks. And we started utilizing the opportunity of being in a residential studio to do different experiments. The acoustic for *A Farewell to Kings* was recorded outdoors, and all of the woodblock and percussion sounds that Neil used were recorded outdoors at the same time. You can hear them echoing off the other buildings, and you can hear the birds tweeting. Because I think we would do it early in the morning; we would experiment with all kinds of wacky things. They had a big echo room there, an acoustic room. It was a really interesting kind of immersion course into country life in Britain, being at this farm, having this whole attitude of having people come in to cook these hearty British meals for us and just getting to

learn a different culture by working there with these wacky, interesting characters of Rockfield."

The sessions for the new album took place in July of '77, right after the band's first UK tour the previous month. Says Alex, "everything else before that had been done in Toronto. We did the short tour, the first time for us in England, then I think came home, then went back. It was so exciting to go to the country where we really felt our musical roots were from, with those progressive bands, and even further back to those bands from the '60s; it's kind of the heart of modern rock music.

"Monmouth was quite an experience, because it's basically a farm. We were surrounded by sheep and farm smells and that sort of thing. And back in those days we used to work the stupid hours where it would gradually get later and later, and you'd get up later and later. So eventually we were getting up five o'clock in the afternoon and having breakfast and then in the studio until seven or eight the next morning. But it was really a great experience, so different. You know, even the lighting is different. They use different kinds of gas bulbs in all their lighting, so there's a different look to everything there. You feel like you're somewhere quite different. At least that was my impression back then. And of course the architecture and the countryside. . . .

"Then we went to London to mix at Advision. And again that was such a treat staying in London for three weeks or something, to mix. So

we were going out to the pubs, hitting all the great Indian restaurants in the area, a really, really fun experience. And musically we were, I don't know . . . going to a new level. We still had some of the longer songs like *Cygnus X-1* and *Xanadu*, but we were getting a little more melodic and a little more dynamic. There's *Closer to the Heart, Farewell to Kings*, both with the use of the acoustics with the three-piece hard rock. Six songs . . ." says an amused Alex to himself, presumably looking at the back cover for the first time in a long time.

Each of those six songs possesses a somewhat timeless and rarified air. The title track begins with renaissance-styled acoustics and then drifts sumptuously on languid power chords, broken from reverie by progressive bits with inventive fills. *Xanadu* is sequenced perfectly after it, possessing the same charm, the same pleasant lilt of a power trio playing attentively, subtly, save for the moderately savage heavy breaks. There are synthesizers, new tinkly percussion gizmos, bass pedals . . . this album marked a pronounced up-ratchet in the accoutrement department.

The enduring 11-minute opus known as *Xanadu* (inspired by Samuel Taylor Coleridge's *Kubla Khan*) would also promulgate the rise of double-neck guitars and basses. "Well, I always thought it was cool that Jimmy Page had one," says Alex. "I was such a Jimmy Page fan. I thought maybe I would like to have one, and I thought that we could really utilize it. There were some songs that had 12-string in them, so it became necessary to have one; with *Xanadu*, the 12-string played such an important role. And Geddy got a double-neck. And then in probably 80% of the pictures I've

seen of me, it's with that fucking guitar [laughs]. And you use it for two songs. It's the same thing with Jimmy Page; most of the pictures you see of him are with his double-neck. It's unusual, and people like it."

Geddy affirms that "the double-neck was all *Xanadu*, the reason we started using double-necks," but then corrects himself. "Actually, it might have been *A Passage to Bangkok* before that, because I played rhythm guitar in the middle section while Alex soloed, and I used bass pedals to supply the bottom end. So I think that's when I first got a double-neck. But *Xanadu* is the song that we really both utilized them in, just so I could go back and play a couple of guitar bits. Because I used to play rhythm guitar in the middle section of *Xanadu* as well."

Of note, Geddy's double-neck was heralded at the time as the first double-neck Rickenbacker, constructed in L.A. specifically for Rush. As mentioned, Neil bulked up as well, speaking in the press of "keyboard percussion" and a whole array of tubular bells and chimes.

Side two of the original vinyl of **A Farewell to Kings** kicks off with *Closer to the Heart*, which would become perhaps tied with *Tom Sawyer* and *The Spirit of Radio* in the pantheon of the band's signature pieces. Deceptively a ballad, and fondly consumed by ducat-relinquishing crowds in that sublime spirit, the song, of course, contains sneaky dollops of fast sections and progressive bits. Later the band, live, would add a reggae-tinged crowd participation piece and then ride it high for the close in similar manner to *The Big Money*. Neil has said that, lyrically, the song offers solutions to the concerns raised within the title track, and indeed the lyrics of the two songs link up seamlessly. Additionally, *Closer to the Heart*, with its chimes, is quite evocative of a Christmas carol, fitting

in that its hit status was most intense during the Yuletide season of '77.

Madrigal is the album's true ballad and is the only track for the record not played live (as a side note, *Xanadu* was previewed live in England). *Cinderella Man* (lyrics by Geddy) contrasts acoustic and electric dynamically in a manner consciously addressed in the Rupert Hine years, with songs like *Roll the Bones*. It would serve an encore track on the tour. Space tale *Cygnus X-1* closes the album with rhythmic aplomb — this one might be viewed as the evil stepchild of *Xanadu*. It is virtually the same length, but it seems to fly by a bit quicker due to its *Necromancer*-like malevolence and aggression. The song had its own themed film when the band was on tour as well as extra technological considerations with respect to instrumentation.

The tour for **A Farewell to Kings** was particularly grueling, so much so that the band dubbed it the Drive til You Die tour. Commencing in August of '77, the band executed a particularly detailed western Canadian swing that kicked off five solid months throughout America. A sixth solid month, February of '78, was spent playing to twice as much of the UK than half a year before. After two weeks of travel and adjustment of the trousers, the band found themselves in Knoxville, Tennessee, in mid-March for southern dates, breaking for April, then touring middle America in May. These latter dates were essentially considered part of the **Archives** tour, **Archives** being a repackaging of the first three albums as a sort of reintroduction to the band's early works. The lack of promotional support for **Caress of Steel**, as it turned out, would still rankle the band years later, with Geddy on the press trail in '78 saying that one of the prime purposes of **Archives** was to give **Caress of Steel**, a record the boys still believed in, a second life. Geddy also quipped, with a reference to his former face-painted tourmates and their **Originals** album, that fans wouldn't be asked to join anything and that they shouldn't expect Rush army stickers upon the purchase of **Archives**.

"I think it was around **2112**, which became the first headline tour, that we would carry our own stuff," recalls Alex, offering a brief history of the minimal stage dressing up to this point. "We didn't have a great deal. Around the time of **Caress of Steel**, I don't think we had much at all. I think it was just us playing with our lights. Our lighting director Howard Ungerleider has always been very good, very in tune with the band and the music. I think he's probably the best LD there ever was; I think he's just brilliant. So we've relied on that. Eventually, I think we got a mirror ball. That was one of the first effects we had [laughs]; that was pretty big back then. And then slowly we got projectors and started incorporating some pyro flash pots — around the time of **2112**. And then around the time of **Kings**, we had the dry ice and that sort of thing. We'd always try to be leading edge with what we could use to make it more visual."

When asked if, throughout the history of the band, there were ever any ambitious show visuals that had to remain drawing board dreams for any reason, Geddy quipped, "Yes. Probably any show that Howard Ungerleider has ever designed [laughs]. No, there's usually . . . no, I don't know if we've ever gone that route. Sometimes there are huge lighting rigs that he may have wanted that just were not reasonable. Depends. In

the early days, obviously we had financial restrictions, and as we got more successful we were only really restricted by what we thought was over the top. Or, because of the fact that in kind of our middle period, when we were playing all around the world, we needed to have a show that was flexible enough to put into a small venue, if we were going to mainland Europe or something. We wanted to have some flexibility. But we always brought an ambitious video projection system with us, one way or another. Some of them were more successful than others."

Support for the Drive til You Die tour came from dependable home-town friends Max Webster, as well as AC/DC (perhaps you've heard of them?), April Wine, Blue Öyster Cult, Cheap Trick, City Boy, Hush, Lynx, Tom Petty and the Heartbreakers, the Pat Travers Band and UFO. Over in the UK, the backup was Tyla Gang, while the **Archives** tour included The Babys, Head East, The Pat Travers Band again and finally Uriah Heep, headliner for Neil's first show in '74, now floundering after the split with vocalist David Byron.

"Yes, they were funny," begins Alex, cajoled into dredging up the memory of legendary pint-swillers UFO. "We did a show with them, and I remember, it was in Spokane [laughs]. It's amazing that I remember these places. And I just remember looking over, and they were all stand-ing there in these robes. But they just got these granny robes, and they had the big fluffy slippers, and they were really taking the piss out of us." If you recall, Rush for a short time wore "Chinese housecoats," as Alex calls them, exhibiting a rare period of wardrobe synchronicity.

"Man, those dates we did with UFO . . . ugh, I don't know how we survived them," continues Alex. "Just the level of drinking! Every night with them was a riot, but it was just like heavy, heavy drinking. Those guys would start drinking . . . they'd show up for soundcheck, but they never did a soundcheck. They'd show up for soundcheck so they could start drinking, you know, because they knew the booze was at the gig, and it was free. We'd always see them before we went on. They would go back to their dressing room, change and always come up to our dressing room before we went on. And they were tanked by that time! But they were just the kind of fun drunks. Pete Way especially; he was just so hilar-ious the whole time."

Neil claims never to have assumed the drum throne under the influ-ence — but sick as a dog, yes. "I remember being on stage in Houston one night with a bucket beside me to throw up in between songs, just hoping I could get through the song and just at least, you know, throw up in the dark. I mean, there's no question of not doing it. There are

12,000 people out there. It's the only job in the world that you can't call in sick on, that I can think of! Really, think about it. People do, but for us, for all of us, if there's any chance at all that we can pull it off, we do it. And we very rarely cancel the show. None on the last two tours that I can think of [here he's speaking of **Test for Echo** and **Vapor Trails**], and maybe one tour, where Geddy's voice would just be gone completely. Maybe one show a tour we would postpone. But there's one thing about getting older. You do get more consistent health-wise, or we have."

But as alluded to, the **Farewell to Kings** tour was particularly grinding. "Yes, we just felt like we were just dying out there on the road," recalls Geddy. Hence the grim nickname of the tour. "It was incredibly difficult, very frustrating. Because at one point, I think we did 17 or 18 one-nighters in a row, and each with a minimum of a 200-mile drive after the gig. So we would just gig and drive, gig and drive, gig and drive. And we were just insane by the end of it; we were just nuts. And we would do anything to keep ourselves awake. We've all talked about certain things that change you. That tour changed us. Making **Hemispheres** changed us. **Grace Under Pressure** changed us. Those were records that were so difficult to make, and that tour was so difficult to do, that they took a piece out of you. You weren't the same person at the end of those experiences that you were at the beginning. Not all bad, but some bad, you know?"

And who dealt with it best? "Well, Pratt was always very in control," continues Geddy. "He's probably the most in-control person. Because he would disappear into his books; he was always very disciplined. He knew when he had too much to drink, or he knew when he had done too

much of this or the other; he knew when it was time to go to bed. And he was very reliable like that. In that sense, he was a good role model because he knew his limits. Alex never knew his limits [laughs]. And I was kind of a conservative guy, so I would never get that out of control. But it would happen.

"And that lifestyle lends itself to that. Because you don't know what side is up after a while. After six months of touring like that, you're just running on fumes basically. It's all about the gig, getting to the gig, being in shape for the gig. I would have to say because our gigs are so hard to play, and the playing was so important to us, it kept us in line. We allowed ourselves some indulgences, but we knew the worst thing that could happen was to blow the gig — to not play well, to not be able to sing well.

"And I really had a lot of trouble on that tour staying healthy. I would get colds a lot in those days and be singing through colds. I mean, we would rarely cancel gigs. It just wasn't something done, that we canceled gigs. I think our saving grace of anything to do with our band has always been the fact that we really embarrass easily, and we don't want to go out there and embarrass ourselves in front of a crowd of people. Playing is so important to us that it's really kept us straight, or as straight as we need to be. I would say that that was an overriding, very helpful thing, our sort of professional instincts."

"It was called Drive til You Die because that's all we were doing," says Neil, adding his impression of this particularly tough slog, comparing those days to now. "We were certainly under a state of exhaustion. We were still driving ourselves in the camper van, and we would do all these one-nighters in a row across the southwest, driving 300, 400 miles ourselves, taking shifts, and then play a headline set night after night. Oh, yeah, we were in an awful state; it was soul-destroying.

"But even now, I'm constantly short of sleep, just because of the way I've done it the last couple times with motorcycling all the time; I want to get up early and get out there. But when your day peaks at 11 o'clock at night, the time doesn't work out. So I would be backstage in my warm-up room with an alarm clock and just, 'OK, 20 minutes,' and sleep for 20 minutes literally [laughs]. It's a question of adaptation really. If you can't deal with lack of sleep and irregular hours and diet and all that stuff, you won't survive. But, oh, right back to the earliest days, we would be going without enough sleep and too much traveling and bad food and all of that stuff."

Back on the ledger books, however, things were humming along, so much so that the band, somewhat ironically, got themselves some wheels to die for. Alex hooked up with a Jaguar XJS, while Neil opted for a Mercedes SL, Geddy a Porsche Targa. It wasn't necessarily an extravagant indulgence, as halfway through the tour **A Farewell to Kings**, **All the World's a Stage** and **2112** each received its gold record designation in the States (many golds and platinums in Canada were a given), the band finally reaping the benefits of all that deadly driving.

Hemispheres

Rush's proposal for 1978 was to be, in a sense, the more realized of a duality instigated one record previous. In fact, Hemispheres would make no apologies for what was now essentially a string of four records each with a half side or more of lengthy, languished, art rock epics. Still, its tripartite joie de vivre is closest in spirit to its immediate predecessor.

"Yes," agrees Neil, "like Power Windows and Hold Your Fire, Farewell and Hemispheres are very much of a period. And, in fact, they represent a period to themselves. It was A Farewell to Kings where we started with a lot of the textural experimentation. And we took it to its apogee absolutely with Hemispheres, then decided tacitly [laughs] — or, no, vocally — that we wouldn't do that anymore. That Hemispheres was the end, that we didn't want to do side-long pieces, the overblown arranging, anymore. We agreed at the time even then that we were done with that, and we of course moved on come Permanent Waves — more in an evolutionary way, but yet it was more than that."

Comprised of two quite heavy short snappers, a neck-snapper of an instrumental and a full side deemed *Cygnus X-1 Book II — Hemispheres* (just *Hemispheres* on the original record label and *Hemispheres* thereafter), this would be a back-breaker for the band to make but a fast fan favorite for years to come. *Circumstances* is a roiling and rhythmic heavy number containing echoes of Peart's demoralizing time in England as a teenager and into his 20's; it also brings up supposition about the role of fate in our lives. *The Trees* is a tidier, more melodic hard rocker housing a labor-management standoff between the maples and the oaks, a lyric Peart now considers trite. *La Villa Strangiato* is a thrilling instrumental, sort of the deluxe version of the slightly better loved YYZ. And finally there's the title track, a bewildering collection of movements that adopts a tone somewhere between the original *Cygnus X-1* and the more benign *Xanadu*. The overriding theme is one of left-brain/right-brain dichotomy, with classic Greek gods personifying the two realms or characteristics within those spheres.

Geddy jokes that the album had no traditional "last-minute" song on it, because "the whole record was like that," adding that "when we arrived in England to record . . . we had nothing written. We went into

this farmhouse; it was actually a house near Rockfield that we spent, I think, three or four weeks in writing. And we wrote the whole **Hemispheres** album in that house and then moved into Rockfield to start recording. That's why it was such an exceedingly difficult album to record — because we spent weeks writing, and we were experimenting with new keyboards, and it was just a tough record, and it was an ambitious record rhythmically with odd time changes and stuff like that. It's probably the most complex record we've ever made. And when we got to Rockfield finally, after writing this stuff, we wanted to record as much live off the floor as we could, as much in one piece as we could. Even *La Villa Strangiato* we wanted to record as one ten-minute piece. But we were also becoming perfectionists at that point and just didn't like the long pieces we were doing. They started to lose energy, so we finally compromised, and I think we recorded that song in three pieces, and then we glued them together.

"The whole album is the three of us playing together. I mean, all of those albums were done that way. But it's just that we couldn't do the whole ten-minute thing without breaking it up, and getting it to the quality we wanted, without stopping after four minutes. 'OK, take

a breather, let's do the next four minutes, take a breather.' And that's kind of the way we did it. But they were all live. Of course, we added overdubs afterward, doubled guitars and extra stuff. But **Hemispheres** and the records before that were all live.

"It was only in the Peter Collins days that we started recording in a slightly different way. We started making very elaborate demos, and then sometimes the demos would be so good we'd add the drums to the demos, and rerecord certain of our parts, and that became a different way of recording. Technology changed a lot, and that's the way we worked for a long, long time. But now we're tending to go back to live recording again."

More grief was yet to come, says Geddy. "Something else that made that album so difficult was when we got to London to mix it, finally, after months and months of being in the Welsh countryside. We did additional recording and mixing at Advision. We had mixed **Farewell to Kings** there and had such a great experience we just assumed it would be great again. It was also where a lot of our favorite Yes albums had been mixed, so it held a kind of special aura about it.

"We were supposed to have the vocals done by then, in Wales, but we were way late because of how difficult the record was to make. When I went in to do the vocals, I realized that I had not sung any of these things out, with the guys, during the writing process, because we kind of wrote the music, and I would sit down and acoustically sing some of the melodies, and everybody would go 'Yeah, that's going to work, that's going to work, OK.' And we just assumed it would all be fine. So we never really checked the keys that the songs were written in. And when I went to sing them, they were in such difficult keys for me to sing, that's why I'm singing so high on that record.

"And it was just a ball-buster to record! And I remember it being incredibly frustrating, you know, having huge blowouts doing the vocals, with Terry, just because I was so frustrated sometimes, just having to get out of the studio and go for a walk on the streets and cool out. Everything to do with that album was like pulling teeth. It was turning into the never-ending album, a real test of your patience and determination. When we finally got all the vocals down, and then started mixing it at Advision, we couldn't get the mix; everything sounded wrong. And that's when we moved studios again and moved to Trident Studios, where it all came together; it was just the right room for it. But every stage of that record there were unforeseen problems, also worsened by the fact that we were months away from home in England. Our families were becoming just, you know . . . a rumor."

Alex fleshes out the story of the Advision mix. "It was just a nightmare; nothing sounded good. We couldn't get a sense of what was happening sonically. And then finally, after spending two or three weeks, we decided to go home. We hadn't been home in three months, I think, at that point. Let's go home for a week, take a break, get away from this, we'll come back, and we'll go to Trident and mix there. And right away everything was so much more apparent at Trident. But it was a hard record to make. Both the material and the technology were demanding."

This time out, the tour itinerary was once again quite exhaustive, Rush embarking on a nine-month trek (deemed, dauntingly enough, Tour of the Hemispheres) that saw the band play extensively in central Canada and fairly thoroughly in western Canada as well as every crease and corner of America. In late April, Rush did their largest European tour yet, split roughly between the UK and the mainland. What would be the first Paris date ever was canceled due to a fire at the venue. The European tour was accompanied by the unauthorized release of a Dutch-pressed single LP compilation called **Rush Through Time**. Acts called upon in various cities to warm up Rush's crowd included Ambrosia, April Wine, Blackfoot, Blondie, The Boyzz, Cheap Trick, Falcon Eddy, Golden Earring, Good Rats, Granmax, Head East, Kickin', Madcats, Max Webster (for the

European jaunt), Molly Hatchet, the Pat Travers Band, Sad Café, Saxon, Starz, Stillwater, Toto, UFO, Wild Horses and Wireless.

Every track from the album would get presented live, although *Circumstances* would get dropped late in the tour, with *Hemispheres* living on in mercifully shortened form. *The Trees* would have the longest shelf life, with *La Villa Strangiato* living on as well, given its pliability for freedom, abbreviation and segue-ability.

On tour, Alex hit the books. "The first thing that I applied myself to was getting my pilot's license, in 1979. I took my training at Buttonville Airport, but we were on tour so much. So I took all my books with me and did all my studying, and when I came home for those few days off, I'd go to the airport and get a couple of hours in. It took me a year to get my license that way. But it was the first time I really applied myself to something outside of the band that really required a lot of work. And I was really proud of the fact."

Finally, Alex explains why the trend had always been for the band to play only scattered shows around numerous, regular shows for the UK and Germany specifically. "Well, we went back and did a couple of shows in Sweden. We played Stockholm and Gothenburg a few tours later. But, yes, Britain was always the main thing, and in Germany, you know, there were so many American and Canadian troops stationed there — even British troops — that you could play a place like Frankfurt and do good business and have a good crowd of 10,000, 11,000 people. That's not so

much the case now. Even the last time we were there in '92, I think, those military bases, a lot of them, are closed down, so you're playing more to a German audience, which is really what you want, but there's not that many of them. So it was because there was such a broader audience in those places. And we played Paris as well, later. We tried to play there a few times before, but something always came up. We've always done a gig in Rotterdam, but that's like playing in England. Everybody speaks perfect English in Holland. They're sort of in between, I guess, the Germans and the Brits. But I think we were just much more popular in Britain than we were anywhere else on the continent."

Permanent Waves

Released January 1st, 1980, Permanent Waves is not
one of those albums that is part of any neat and tidy
Rush pairing. Celebrating the complexity of its two
predecessors, it also eschews the egregiously long
songs found on each one of the preceding four albums.
And actually the thing's a song short, at 35 minutes, as
if one of those regular last-minute songs forgot to
present itself.

With respect to the title, both Alex and Neil had
remarked that it was a statement of defiance against
the hype of music's current new wave. On another
tack, the original title had been Wavelength, with plans
to incorporate in the graphics actual EKGs of the band
playing, evoking some sort of statement along a
human versus technology theme.

Natural Science (parts of it plundered from a mass of ideas called Uncle Tounouse), at nearly ten minutes, is the album's multimovement timepiece. Dark and often heavy, the track finds Neil speaking of science's beauty and then humanity's hubris-filled attempts to control it, annihilation the only outcome, unless enlightenment prevails. Jacob's Ladder is slightly less involved but perhaps even darker. Lyrically, in fact, it is a description of a weather phenomenon (Neil is a professed weather nut) in which the clouds break and the resulting shaft of sunlight resembles a ladder to the heavens. Odd man out on the record is Different Strings, a hugely under-rated ballad for the band, sophisticated textures and melodies marking a step forward indeed. Comments Alex, "There's usually one song per album that is produced in such a way that we'll never play them live. Madrigal is one of those, so is Different Strings."

And after that, all that is left is a trio of short, sharp, tight, perky rockers, Entre Nous (trotted out to no avail as the second single) being the most informal, Free Will and The Spirit of Radio serving dutifully as sterling Rush classics and perennial live staples. The Spirit of Radio is a dramatic pastiche of musics, in emulation of the central theme — that radio once was about freedom to choose rather than mercantile exploitation of narrowed, contrived (imagined?) market segments. That title was also the slogan of local Toronto radio station CFNY. Finally, Freewill swings effortlessly despite its use of odd time signatures (mostly 13/4) as well as a pumping 4/4.

As a general observation, the production on **Permanent Waves** is exemplary. Despite the band's exhaustive, never-ending search for new

— and, according to the band, perfect or accurate — sounds, an arguable perfection is achieved right here, Terry Brown arriving at a bracing balance between bass, treble and light blue clarity. And the band play ecstatically, making Broon (a.k.a. Terry Brown) look good and vice versa.

But Neil would heartily disagree that anything close to a perfect drum sound is captured on **Permanent Waves** or any of the albums from around that time. In fact, perfection, logically, is a never-ending pursuit, an ever-receding horizon. "No, in the early days, both the equipment and the engineering was so limited, and everything had a damp, muffled kind of sound. Again, what you learn . . . I didn't tune drums as well then, so I might have to put damping on them. Or they didn't have the singing tonality that I learned how to get out of drums later, both through technique and tuning ability and head choices. All of that kind of stuff you learn and develop as you go along; it becomes part of your voice. I didn't have it then, really. I was groping towards how drums should sound and how I should play them. But by no means was I a master of it. So, no, I don't think they are natural sounding, those albums. It just wasn't possible. It's still not possible, really. It's still something that's being worked towards.

"Anyway, there was a very strong division between **Hemispheres** and **Permanent Waves**," adds Neil with respect now to the compositions enclosed, "even though we still had a lot of long pieces and a lot of extended arrangements and instrumentation and so on. But there was

still a change of attitude. And it was the late '70s, the music we were responding to. *The Spirit of Radio* incorporates stylistically and again, implicitly, what all that was about. There was a huge shift, and from **Permanent Waves**, that set us up to be able to do **Moving Pictures**. That was a complete realization of what we decided to do at the end of **Hemispheres** that was realized with **Moving Pictures**. Very often that's the case; there'll be a whole album's growth necessary to take us to where we're going. And I remember a critic around that time in the '70s saying he just wished he could give us a big kick in the direction we were going. And that was a very nice criticism, you know? And one of the few worthwhile ones I could think of, that we ever received, in terms of criticism. That was really thoughtful. I remember Geddy pointing it out to me, how great that was. Yes, he was acknowledging that we were going in the right direction but it was taking too long. Sorry [laughs]!"

"There are some good songs on there," adds Alex, perusing the back cover of the original vinyl. "*Natural Science* is one of my favorite songs to

play live, at this point. *Jacob's Ladder*, *Entre Nous*, yeah, a lot of those songs. *Spirit of Radio*, *Freewill*, those are really two Rush classics.

"It was the first album we did at Le Studio, Morin Heights, which is in rural Quebec, and it was such a treat to work there. We set up a whole volleyball net/court outside of the front door of the house we were staying at, which is by a lake. We put lights up, the whole thing, so we could come back at two in the morning, when we were finished recording, and play volleyball for a couple of hours — and of course drink and all that stuff. It was really a lot of fun. It was about a mile to paddle or row from the lake to the studio from the house. It was really a great vibe working there. That's before Le Studio became a big complex, so it had a very homey vibe to it. Yael and André Perry [French cuisine, both on-site and through his restaurant La Barratte, at least when Alex was not cooking] were just wonderful people. We had some great dinners; I have very fond memories of it.

"That was a very traditional period. We had just gone from that last

concept thing, **Hemispheres**, and we had been recording in England quite a bit through that period of the '70s. But that one we recorded, like I say, at Le Studio, but we mixed it in England, at Trident. It was an attempt to condense our songs a little bit, be more economical, try to get as much as we could in that four- to five-minute framework rather than eight to 11 minutes."

"That became a regular thing, an obsession," says Geddy, keying in on Alex's mention of volleyball. "That was one of our early introductions to sport activities [laughs]. We'd finish at one in the morning or whatever, and we kind of perfected the art of night volleyball. And we played even in the winter. We'd have a few drinks and get a bit fortified after the session and go out on the volleyball pitch. We built light standards and had it lit so we could play at night. And sometimes we'd even play after dinner a little bit, but then we'd get back into the studio, and our hands would be all swollen from punching this stupid ball [laughs]. We were like . . . I don't know if we should be playing like this, after supper.

"Everything on the **Permanent Waves** record came together in a relatively short period of time," adds Geddy, getting back to the business at hand (of note is the surprising happenstance that this was the first time the band had actual time off between the previous record's tour and the writing for the next album). "In fact, it was one of the most pleasurable and easiest albums for us to record. It was just one of those great writing sessions. At that time, it was still three of us sitting around, throwing ideas together and writing together, in typical garage band style. We would write two songs, rehearse them, take them into the studio and lay down live backing tracks. Everything just clicked. Morin Heights was beautiful, and the engineer was terrific. It all kind of came together in a very quick and spontaneous way which I think is reflected in the songs. Subsequently, we've tried to maintain that over the years."

Getting specific, Geddy talks about *Natural Science* and how it's been transformed 20 years later. "That's one of my favorite songs. It's one of those songs that kind of went away in our live show for many years. And when we brought it back, we changed the arrangement a bit. There were things in the arrangement that were a little shortchanged in the original song. Like in the second part of the song for the main 'wheels within wheels' part of the song. It's not a traditional song; there's no real verse/chorus/verse/chorus, but I remember certain melodies like that that I felt deserved to appear more than they did, and I thought it would give the song more resonance. So we did those things, and the last section of the song is made shorter than it was in the original version. I felt we had kind of overdone it on the record. So sometimes there's that opportunity to fix a mistake or an arrangement that may be shortchanged in some way. And I think our current version live is the best we've ever played it."

The **Permanent Waves** tour, commencing in mid-January of '80, was preceded by a warm-up tour in August and September of the previous year (FM and Pat Travers as support, Wild Horses at the one UK date) before the fall sessions for the album were to take place. Both *The Spirit of Radio* and *Freewill* were road-tested, without finished guitar solos, while *Jacob's Ladder* was also worked on during soundchecks. The tour proper spanned six months throughout the US and Canada (conspicuously with no Ontario dates) with the final month, June, finding the band playing England — 19 nights out of 22 — with no trek to continental Europe this time out.

For extracurricular fun (and we're talking generally here about activities that would pop up on various or numerous tours), the band and crew would watch hockey games whenever possible (Alex used to quip that soundcheck was going to be late if there was an afternoon game on). Further on that theme, if circumstances allowed it, the band would often take over the local rink and play a game themselves, sometimes with real NHLers (ex-Montreal star Steve Shutt is a friend of the band). This went on for several tours, and in fact sometimes the plan was to take over the ice at the arena they *had just played*, trotting out in full uniform for a quick game during teardown, before driving on to the next city. As

well, there were always racetracks and amusement parks, not to mention backstage rollerskating! For Neil, there were his books (he'd usually devour one every two or three days) and — especially with respect to Geddy — many, many movies, sometimes three a day.

Support for the tour came from Max Webster, Saga and 38 Special, with New Wave of British Heavy Metal stalwarts Quartz called up for duty in England. *Different Strings* and, oddly, *Entre Nous* would not be taken from the album to the stage.

"*Natural Science* is always a real challenge to play live," remarked Alex years later. "There's a lot of intricate, hard playing in it; the tempo's quite upbeat. You sort of step up into it and just go right until the end. So that's always a challenge for all of us. And when we play that well, it really feels great."

Yet again hometown friends Max Webster were called upon to support multiple dates. Max, of course, was the second most prominent Anthem Records act after Rush, they were produced by Terry Brown and in some respects they were Rush-like. Their lyricist occasionally collaborated on Rush songs with Neil, and indeed keyboardist Terry Watkinson was key in teaching Geddy what he knows about the ebonies and ivories. For Max Webster's final album, **Universal Juveniles**, Rush teamed up with the band and roared their way through massive and near-immovable Max epic *Battle Scar*, a song the band knew all too well because Max had been playing it live. In fact, Neil was already playing it, having by this time adopted the habit of warming up to the last few songs of Max's set shortly before Rush was to take over.

"Yeah, behind Sticksy," explains Alex, referring to consummate Max drummer Gary McCracken. "There was a scrim that went across the stage. Max was out there. Neil's kit was directly behind Sticksy, and he'd go up, and that was his warm-up. He'd go up and play the last few songs with them. I think he might have done it a couple times years later with Primus, but it was a nightly thing with Max. We did so many dates with them.

"In fact, we were on tour when Kim [Mitchell — lead vocals, guitars] had had enough and decided to go home. I remember pulling into that gig, and all the guys were sitting on the grass, and they looked so

despondent. 'What happened?' 'Kim's had enough. He can't take it anymore. He went home.' 'He went home?' 'Yeah, he went home. He was on
a flight this morning and went home.' So they were stuck there. And we
took them to Europe and all over America. They were really starting to
catch on in the States too. They were really developing a following where
people were becoming familiar with their music. They were starting to
develop a fan base. But I think Kim . . . it's a little much for him, to travel that much and be away; it was a lot of pressure, and I don't think he
dealt with pressure that well. I think he was much happier to be here
where everything was a given. At least that was my impression then."

"Yeah, at that time, my drums were under a tent on the stage," clarifies Neil about his odd warm-up routine, "so I could go up under there
and hang around and listen to the band do the song. And sometimes I
would just play along with Max Webster songs. Nobody could hear me,
I don't think. I would be backstage and then go in. No one knew I was
there. It was a tarp, and it would hang off this rack system I had with
all my bells and blocks, so the tarp went over that." It must have at least
wiggled a bit, no? "Oh, I'm sure it did. But I don't think anyone was
looking at the covered-up drum set to wiggle [laughs]. I remember also
one of their songs had the Max Webster dancing in it, and we used to
put weird costumes on and go and dance around the stage for 30 seconds. You would hear the call backstage, 'Come on, it's Max Webster
dancing coming up!' And everyone would fashion costumes out of
whatever we could find and go up there."

Moving
Pictures

Moving Pictures would prove to be one of those Rush records that is the realization of a vision. And Alex, Geddy and Neil would be roundly rewarded for it, the record at this juncture sitting at quadruple platinum in the States ("I remember that blowing our minds," says Geddy) and likely forever, like Machine Head for Deep Purple and like Paranoid for Black Sabbath, to be the catalog's most brisk seller, given the strange herd-like vagaries of human behavior. In other words, it will never be a case that everybody who wants it will have it. Rather, any new fan of the band will start here, and those not dedicated beyond certain parameters will stop here. Expand on that thought some more, and what you have is the Rush album owned by, or likely to be owned by, folks who don't particularly consider themselves to be fans. Maybe even folks who don't consider much at all.

Hugh Syme was at the height of his comedic powers on this one, presenting to Rush's public a picture of movers moving emotionally moving pictures, the whole scene, as the back revealed, being shot for a motion picture. In addition, the setting for the shoot was Ontario's seat of government, Queen's Park, which featured as part of its entrance three arches, separated by a triple set of pillars.

One can't deny that the explosion of heavy metal's loud and large stature in the UK through the New Wave of British Heavy Metal (America was two years behind the curve, waiting for MTV to push the genre over the top) aided and abetted Rush's up-ratchet to this new and unforeseen level of success, despite the band being so much more than Priest riffs recycled as Maiden riffs. Geddy acknowledged at least a slight effect in the press at the time but echoes the attitudes of his compatriots that Rush only bears a passing resemblance to the heavy metal acts so often mentioned in the same breath.

"There are two terms that are often confused for each other," noted Geddy, years later, when asked to consider Rush's relationship to heavy metal. "One is hard rock, and one is heavy metal. I've always thought of us as progressive hard rock, owing more to bands like The Who and Zeppelin than bands like Black Sabbath. To me, Black Sabbath was metal; The Who were rock. Zeppelin were metalish rock and kind of began a whole style of rock. They really invented metal as far as I was concerned. But you can go back farther than them to Blue Cheer and say that they

invented metal, because they were really doing that kind of thing before anybody was, even though they could barely play. So I would say that we are a mixture of those influences. I think we tried to stay more on the rock side of metal through our career. But we have moments where we indulge in metal because it can be a glorious, raw medium. But I don't think we were ever very gothic about our metal [laughs], whereas a lot of metal bands are very gothic."

Consensus is that **Moving Pictures** is the record on which Geddy toned down his patented high shriek. "You know, as the music changed, the desire to shriek changed," explains Geddy. "I think I can still shriek if the music requires it. I have no conceptual adverse feelings about it [laughs]. As the music changed, it became more interesting for me to write melodies as opposed to shrieking. It was basically used for cutting through the density of the music. And sometimes we would write without any consideration for what key we were in in the early days. And I would find myself with 12 tracks recorded in a key that was real tough to sing in, so I didn't have a choice at that point. Rerecord the record in a different key, or just go for it.

"I bought it at Kresge's," laughs Lee on coming up with his signature yowl in the first place. "I keep it downstairs in my studio for when I need it. Lifetime guarantee."

Moving Pictures contains — strangely enough heaped to one side — four hearty hits. YYZ (call letters for Toronto's Pearson International

Airport) is the band's most recognizable and celebrated instrumental. It is short, obliquely humorous, fired to a smart, tart sheen in the crucible of rhythm, and it is swimmingly enjoyable. *Red Barchetta* benefits from a similar enthusiastic élan, its sweet melodies balancing nicely the carnality of a true power trio celebration. The track, musically and lyrically, sets off visions of rural road racing (the effect is deliberately cinematic), enveloping the listener in feelings of oneness and nostalgia, even if the tale is in fact a futuristic one in which the car, like the guitar in **2112**, has been outlawed. *Limelight* intensifies the previous track's idea of oneness, ironically, despite the lyric's paean to self-imposed, deliberate isolation. The music wins.

But it is the album's opening track that would propel the album to lofty heights, *Tom Sawyer* swirling into the camera eye with vortextual sounds cycloning a slow and deliberate 4/4 beat. Its ebbs and flows are legion, its totality Rush's ambassador of song. "I love that song, and I never get tired of playing it," muses Geddy. "The fact that it is so popular still just confuses the hell out of me. I love the fact that it begins with such a great backbeat, and there's this kind of faux rap part. To me,

the song is just about innocence more than anything, and I think that comes through. And it still holds through somehow; the slightly inscrutable lyrics still deliver that message to people, and people identify with it, and they dig it. And it's got this weird middle part. And if you can get away with that in a popular song . . . geez, it's a major victory." Interestingly, *Tom Sawyer* actually began life as a melody Geddy would play on synthesizer at soundchecks, a modus operandi that produced many a bit, especially when soundchecks began to be recorded to catch such musical manna.

Neil confirms that *Tom Sawyer* is one of the tougher Rush songs to pull off properly from a drum standpoint. Only these days for him, it's not so much any of the purely technical aspects, such as the quick hi-hat pattern placed on an open architecture and quite slow beat. "It is, but it's more so due to feel, always, the subtleties of music. The more sophisticated your knowledge and tastes become, then the subtler are the things you're looking for. And there's a fundamental feel thing that I'm always seeking in it and in all songs. It's the reason I keep listening to live tapes on days off on the road, to make sure I'm nailing that tempo. A small shift in feel affects everything so much, and I'll hear where, well, Geddy's having to sing that line too fast, I should pull the tempo

back a bit and let it breathe. There are subtleties like that that are hard-won, to nail that every night on stage.

"I was watching a movie called *The T.A.M.I. Show*, which is one of my earliest influences, from '65. And it had everybody from Chuck Berry to James Brown to Leslie Gore to the Beach Boys to the Rolling Stones, who headlined. And I noticed the bands with their own drummers and all that, of course; they're playing live on TV, they're all a little bit speedy and the singers are getting a little breathless. It's subtle; I don't mean that everything was raging fast. But it was just on edge. Whereas Hal Blaine, who played in the orchestra that was backing up all the singers and all that . . . the tempo was just perfect, just laid right down, you know?

"So there's a hard-won mastery of a guy like Hal Blaine who can do that, all the time, anywhere, as opposed to seeking that and trying to achieve it, recognizing it even, those kinds of subtleties. So again a long-winded answer to your question, but it's that kind of a subtle, overall consistency in the feel that I'm looking for.

"To me, a lot of it is ambition that makes me accomplish things," says Neil. "The drive factor. I really want to play the drums, so I'll put the time in it takes to play the drums. I really want to write a book, so I'll spend a year writing a book, and make it the focus of my life and reward of its own, a daily, satisfying work in progress. It's a matter of character. Once

somebody said, 'No failures of talent, only failures of character.' Those are character issues."

The *Tom Sawyer* lyric is wonderful, the definition of enigmatic, and, incidentally, a cogent precursor to that of *New World Man*. It was the first collaboration between Neil Peart and Max Webster lyricist Pye Dubois, and it paints a piecemeal portrait of an edgy, cynical outsider who just may find good and have it found within him. The working title of the piece before Pye handed his bits over to Neil was *Louis the Lawyer* (often miscited as *Louis the Warrior*). "Pye's method is that he just kind of sends me pages of scribbles, and I impose order on them," says Neil. "So it's a perfect meeting of personalities in that he dwells in an imagistic universe and an impressionistic universe and expresses it as such, whereas I live in a much more ordered universe and impose that structure and rhythm and parallel construction on it. I think right from that foundation it's a collaboration of personalities as much as it is of words. Because I'll tend to . . . for example, I'll start with the way he set up the framework for a song like *Force Ten*, and I'll respond to that. I'll start creating images in his voice, as it were, just because that's the character of the piece. And I adapt it like a language. I translate my thoughts into his kind of images or his images into my kind of language, and it becomes a very kind of interwoven, interpersonal collaboration."

Geddy speaks of his own necessary collaboration with Neil on the process of phrasings, turning Neil's musings into something rhythmically sound, and linguistically possible, within the context of the song at hand. "I just think the style changed over the years, but it's not quite as simple

as that. In the early years, the music was ambitious and adventurous and, yes, sometimes the lyrics were unwieldy, but it didn't seem to be a problem in the context of the bombast we were throwing together. But of course, as songs became more melody-oriented and less of a furious onslaught, the requirements lyrically and melodically changed as well. Neil's great to work with in that regard. After the first draft of lyrics are given to me, obviously I have to shape them into a melodic thing. And I have to feel comfortable with them. And if I don't sound comfortable, it's obvious. So the two of us have always worked closely in that regard."

Side two of the album — or the back three tracks if your mind has ordered the album from the CD source — evokes the snap, crackle and pop of **Permanent Waves**. *The Camera Eye* is an 11-minute battle between barbed riffs from Alex and tidal synthesizers from Geddy. *Witch Hunt*, the record's production piece and the most reworked and fretted-over song on the album, introduces the three-part *Fear* trilogy from the vantage point of the third part. Lyrically, it is a poetic indictment of mob mentality; musically, it is Alex at his most sinister.

Vital Signs closes the picture show, continuing the softly pulsing legacy of exploring what can be called exotic, technology-steeped reggae, a slight and side preoccupation began one record previous, to be revisited on **Signals**, double that on **Grace**. "Usually on every album there's one song that we write spontaneously, just at the last minute, and that's the one for that album," says Geddy of *Vital Signs*. "And those songs usually end up taking us in a totally different direction, as that one did. It's kind of a precursor for us getting more involved with sequencers. And it's a last-minute tune. I love those last-minute tunes, because you write them and record them in a short period of time, and it's kind of minimal brain work

— lots of spontaneity; you just kind of go for it — and it ends up being a lot of fun."

"In *Vital Signs*, I wanted an electro sound for that one verse of it," adds Neil. "So, yes, **Moving Pictures** I used electronic snare for the first time; I must have had pads to play that on. Before that, **Permanent Waves** still has a lot of organic percussion on it, no electronics."

"**Moving Pictures** was just a wonderful record to make," adds Alex. Of note, the tentative plan was to do another live album (indeed, eight UK shows were recorded on the last tour), but **Moving Pictures**, fortunately for all, happened instead. "The vibe was so positive and so great in the studio; we were having just so much fun. And the songs really, I think, reflect that. We had the benefit of taking some time off to write. We went up to Peterborough, Stony Lake. We parked ourselves at a cottage for about a month, and we wrote all the stuff up there. So again we were prepared, prior to going into the studio, although there was always a little bit of room to do stuff in the studio, like *Vital Signs*. Sometimes we wrote some songs while we were there, certainly fleshing out and developing parts. It was always fun to leave some room to be spontaneous. For that album, we had gone through this whole period of writing concept pieces and longer songs. By the time we reached **Moving Pictures**, the format had changed quite a bit. I mean, there were still a couple of long songs on that album, but we were writing in a different mode. We were trying to be more economical with our parts. And there is a great vibe to **Moving Pictures**. We had a lot of fun making that record, at Morin Heights again. It was a great winter. **Moving Pictures** has a freshness to it that has passed the test of time; I think some of our strongest material is on that record."

"Alex started getting really heavily into model airplanes," says Geddy, offering further glimpses into Rush's release valves during writing and recording. "It started, I think, when we were writing **Permanent Waves**, in a little farmhouse out of the city [Neil wrote in a separate cottage a quarter mile from the main compound; there an Arthurian epic for that album was planned, then scrapped], and that's when he first started experimenting with these flying machines. And even Terry Brown got into it. In fact, we had a lot of fun. In August of '80, writing **Moving Pictures**, we were working on Ronnie Hawkins' farm out near Stony Lake, and Alex was really into these remote-control airplanes. He would spend hours building them.

"And, of course, they would always go haywire, where they would get up too high or lose control or something. And I remember there was one that went completely haywire and ended up crashing and exploding on the top of Ronnie Hawkins' truck, put a big hole in the top of it [laughs]. And then Terry Brown had this fantastic, this giant one, this giant plane he had been working on. It was so big that you had to have this kind of tether so that it would fly around in circles. And it had a huge engine on it. And I remember he finally cranked it up, and, man, it took off! And suddenly we all had to hit the deck! It was like this charge went out, and everybody is diving for the ground, and poor Broon is holding onto this thing going around in circles. He had to hold onto it until it finally ran out of gas. He's going around and around and around [laughs], and he was completely dizzy. Finally, the plane ran out of gas and landed. And he basically fell over in the grass. He was completely dizzy; it was hilarious [laughs].

"And we continued that at Morin Heights. Alex, and in fact Tony Geranios, who is also known as Jack Secret, started working on rockets at Morin Heights, and we would have these rocket launches, sometimes at dinner, sometimes at breakfast. I remember one time he launched one in the backyard at Morin Heights, and the thing just took off the wrong way completely and missed exploding in Alex's brand-new Mercedes by inches. It was always great fun. Sometimes Alex would fly the planes, and he got into water planes at Morin Heights, because they had a lake. And he would land it in the water and take off from the water."

With success in full stride, Rush vowed to tour less insistently, planning family breaks each month. Still, the **Moving Pictures** tour, and the subsequent and similar-in-set **Exit . . . Stage Left** tour, would stretch from February '81 (at which time **2112** would receive its platinum certification in the States, the first for the band; **All the World's a Stage** would follow suit in March), with a break for three months in the summer, through to December 22 of the same year. Moreover, there was an America-only warm-up tour spanning most of September 1980, with Saxon in tow, where *Limelight* and *Tom Sawyer* were market-tested, both with quicker tempos. These warm-up stints also served as an opportunity to rehearse the larger set of new songs to be presented on the major swing. Of note, it was just after the warm-up tour that recording the album would take place — writing was done at Stony Lake in the summer of '80, and recording at Le Studio from October to December, spanning two seasons, the warm, Indian summer-type fall and the typical snowy conditions of a rural Quebec winter.

For the tour proper, the faithful Midwest would see the band first, followed by central Canada, all compass points of America again, capped by a couple of western Canadian dates in late June, then Minnesota and Wisconsin in July. "It's a pretty playable record," comments Alex, and so everything from the album was played save for *Witch Hunt*, which would

be added subsequently, when the *Fear* trilogy became complete. Alex, years later, would say that "the solo in *Limelight* is probably my favorite solo to play, and if I feel I've really got the fluidity nailed then it's very, very satisfying personally. The whole thing is just very elastic, and it's not always easy to get everything to be very circular from one part to the next. But when it happens, it's really a treat."

Neil's drum solo was inserted into *YYZ*, where it would stay for two tours; *Working Man* received a reggae intro. Support on the tour, which featured back-projected film, pyro and dry ice, came mainly from FM and Max Webster, with Goddo, Ian Hunter and Saga featured at select shows. All told, the band played to 905,000 fans through 79 shows.

"When **Moving Pictures** came out, and we went on tour, that's when everything changed," says Alex. "Really up to this whole period, even with **Permanent Waves**, we were still . . . we were headlining pretty much everywhere, but not big halls, and we would still do some special guest gigs for bigger gigs, but it wasn't until **Moving Pictures** came out that we were a solidly headlining arena kind of band. That was really the big turning point. We were still in debt up until this point. And it wasn't until **Moving Pictures** came out that we could actually get ourselves out of debt and that we were offered to re-sign, renegotiate, redo our deal. That's when a lot of those sorts of worries were dispelled. So, yeah, we went to the next level of playing big gigs and more radio airplay specifically with *Tom Sawyer* and *Limelight*."

Exit . . . Stage Left

The Exit . . . Stage Left tour (if such distinction from the Moving Pictures tour can be said to be valid) would begin in late October of '81, the band covering England in detail as well as Germany, with a side trip to Rotterdam. Then in late November, with only a week's transition from the overseas experience, it was quickly back into the American south with a swing up to Hartford and East Rutherford, New Jersey (two nights each), to temporarily close ranks.

The tour, of course, was in support of the band's second double live album, released in October, in time for the trip overseas. Ads for the album stressed the live set's technological superiority due to digital mastering, a technique also applied to **Moving Pictures**. "That one was an attempt to kind of overexaggerate how perfect you could make a live album," remarks Geddy. "There was a lot of meddling with the tapes and trying to make sure we had the best performances. We also made a conscious effort to pull down the audience a bit and emphasize the music. In the end, I think we recorded a fairly sterile live record. So, yes, that would entail the most tinkering of any of the live albums. We played around with making sure things were in time, snipping bits of time here and there. It turned into a bit of a nightmare of mixing and perfecting. And that was, as with **All the World's a Stage**, most of us being involved, although I think Neil tuned out pretty early in the process." Neil, to his credit, admitted in the press, enthusiastically and without apology, to the odd repair, supposing that all would run easier if he, Alex and Geddy were perfect.

Highlight relief detailing on the album includes the serenade intro to *Jacob's Ladder*, the huge singalong on *Closer to the Heart* (given the nod in the liner notes, with a credit to the Glaswegian Chorus — this was from the **Permanent Waves** tour), Alex's classical guitar piece *Broon's Bane*, Geddy's "vocals" in *La Villa Strangiato* and finally the amusing cover art, which pastiches key visuals from all of the band's previous cover graphics.

Interestingly, all three of the guys have professed in the press an animosity toward live albums, Neil, at the time, even going so far as to say that he didn't think Rush would be making any more of them!

Signals

Signals summarily shocked the fanbase and the critics at the time, but it has now become a love it/hate it album — fans and critics love it, and the boys, well . . . give them some time, they'll come around.

"Certainly, on Signals, there was a conflict, I think, between the guitar and the keyboards we were using," says Alex. "For me, that's always been a bit of a sore spot, that record. Because I think there's good material on there, but I think the production on it is lacking. To me, that record doesn't sound that great, from a guitar point of view. We were just starting to really get into keyboards, and I don't think we were well balanced on that record. And I think that's part of the reason we had decided to move on, in terms of what producer we were going to work with. We wanted to get a little more of an influence from other people."

Yet balanced against the astringent, urgent, intransigent tones of the records that followed, the production is downright plush, blended, creamy. But, of course, it is this way because of all the guitar-emulating keyboards, in stark contrast to the fiery and very real guitar verve of **Moving Pictures**. *Subdivisions* and *New World Man* are majestic Rush classics, and a strong secondary flank of momentous live magic could be sprung from the likes of *The Analog Kid*, *Digital Man* and *Countdown*.

"There was a whole movement at that time," puts forth Geddy as background to the Rush revolt at hand. "There was Midge Ure's band, Ultravox. I think we were influenced a lot by those kinds of bands at the time; they seemed to bring keyboards into it in a very cool way. There are also records produced by Trevor Horn during that period, although that might have come a little bit later, that were very interesting. I think we also got more interested in production, at least from my point of view. I mean, if you were to analyze the history of our band, I think you could say that the first period marked a band developing as players. And as time moved on and we got more proficient as players, that came to surface in a very obvious way on albums like **Hemispheres** and so forth, where the records are very overtly complex. And then we got into this period with keyboards where we started thinking more in terms of making records and producing records. So really **Signals**, **Power Windows** and **Hold Your Fire** marked a shift from being players to producers. And we first got into the idea of adding things to our music that were not easy to reproduce live — our albums became productions. And I would say the last period focuses less on that and more on songwriting.

"Keyboards are a necessary evil to me," says Geddy when asked about his skills as a keyboardist. "I don't take any great pride in my ability to play the keyboards, because I'm not a great keyboard player. I have an arsenal of sounds, and that's really what keyboards represent to me: sounds and textures.

"As far as drums go, I'm finding my way around drum programming pretty well, so it's fun to do that. It's always nice to put drums together without a drummer; it makes life a little easier [laughs]. But when you write by yourself, you have to do those things. You have to be adept at creating a rhythm section and have the keyboards that can give you the

textures and emotional colors that you need to create the kind of song you want to create. It's all part of being more self-sufficient."

"I was listening to all the new wave," adds Neil, contextualizing the motivations for the modern **Signals** sound. "Really, it took every-body a while to find their feet through that time. We were lucky to be a bit younger than most of the other bands and I think more responsive to the music on the radio and in the current style. I was just writing about that period, and I remember a lot of musicians saying [hands on his hips], 'What am I supposed to do? Forget how to play?!' You know, 'I'm not doing this crap!' And, OK, bye. Whereas others . . . think of Peter Gabriel coming out of Genesis and becoming so influential and so vital at the time. Trevor Horn came out of Yes, and look what he spawned, a whole plethora of interesting and vital music of its time. Some people were able to adapt to the modernness without losing anything of what they had."

New technologies were so prevalent on **Signals** that, indeed, Geddy professed to writing tracks like *Subdivisions*, *Chemistry* and *The Weapon* on keyboards. "I guess the first time I wrote a really important part of a song with keyboards was the keyboard line in *Tom Sawyer*," qualifies Geddy, "but in terms of writing a whole song on keyboards the first one was *Subdivisions*." Previously, he had tended to write on bass, which is somewhat curious since most bass players tend to write on guitar, often acoustic.

The album's popcorn-bouncy preview single *New World Man* was writ-ten and recorded nearly "spontaneously" (in two days, to be precise), almost as an afterthought, given that four more minutes were needed to fill up the album. To this day, *New World Man* still races with *Subdivisions* for title as the record's most enduring track. "Well, that was something that started to happen early on," notes Geddy of the last-minute track con-cept. "We always felt that there was one more song we could put on a record. It started way back with **2112**. The song *Twilight Zone* was a song we threw on at the last minute. We wrote it in the studio, recorded it, all over a matter of two days. And that became a tradition for us that we kind

of looked forward to. What's going to be the last-minute song on this record? Because so much of our stuff is rehearsed, planned out, it was nice to have something on each record that was off the cuff. *Vital Signs* was like that too, as was *New World Man*."

Surging and shifting album closer *Countdown* noticeably included a synthesizer solo from Geddy in which Alex might have wandered, albeit obtusely, given the times. Definitely not a favorite of Neil's, the track was inspired by a trip the band took in April of '82 to Cape Canaveral (specifically Red Sector A, the VIP area) to watch the liftoff of the space shuttle *Columbia*. It would be the record's third and last single, and its video would be memorable for its NASA-authorized space footage. Over in the lyric department, Neil spoke of the album as his first that was pointedly about real, ordinary people, their dreams, ideals, environments, a broad theme represented by the title and territorial cover art, art that also addressed the umbrella concept of cold chemistry (science?), which rules all.

Preceding the **Signals** tour proper would be the band's spring training tour for '82, otherwise known as the Tour of the Nadars. The tour was nothing more than a two-week run through the first half of April, hitting the American south. Support came from Riggs (having their 15 minutes of fame based more on the **Heavy Metal** soundtrack album than on their self-titled debut) as well as Krokus, with the now-deceased Rory Gallagher playing one date. Rory was one of Alex's favorite guitarists from the formative years as well as a respected and well-remembered headliner above Rush in the early days.

The actual **Signals** tour, otherwise known as the New World Tour, would be a characteristically long jaunt. Beginning in the central US on September 3rd, 1982 (the record launched a week later), the band would veer west through the States, hitting four of the larger western Canadian

markets on the way. Back in the US in early October, the band would then move on to three triumphant days at home at Maple Leaf Gardens, in mid-November, the Payolas in tow, with the third date being a UNICEF benefit raising $161,560.53. Two weeks later the band made a two-night, sold-out stand at Madison Square Garden. The rest of America would be next, culminating in three Quebec dates in mid-April before a couple weeks off. Along the way, Boston Gardens was a sell-out, with Cleveland, Detroit and Long Island selling out two nights apiece, Chicago three nights. For all of May, it was overseas to the Netherlands, Germany, Belgium and nine dates in the UK, including a four-night stand at Wembley.

Smack in the middle of this tour and the next one would be a five-night stint at New York's Radio City Music Hall, support coming from promising Genesis-steeped neoproggers Marillion. These dates would road-test three tracks from **Grace Under Pressure**, not due out for another six months. "I remember it being a great gig," recalls Geddy with respect to Radio City. "Somebody just suggested it would be a great venue to play, and sometimes you just want to change the way you do things? And we thought, wow, that's neat; I mean, for us to do that kind of venue was really cool, especially because it ended up being more than just a couple of shows. In fact, we're talking about doing it again on this [30th anniversary] tour. I think it's just nice to change things up, plus we needed to warm up a bit for the recording of **Grace**." Interestingly, press at the time had Alex and Geddy eager to get to work on solo albums once the current trek was over, Neil to work on a book of poetry.

Shows on the **Signals** tour began to the happy-go-dumb strains of *The Three Stooges* theme song, an intro track that would be used on the band's subsequent three tours as well. *SCTV*'s Count Floyd ("Ooh, this one's scary!") and archival footage from *Get Smart* would lighten up *The Weapon*

and *New World Man* respectively. *Subdivisions* would have film to underscore its theme of suburban, middle-class alienation. With respect to the tour's set list, the tone was mercilessly modern. Only three selections were trotted out from the first four albums, and no fewer than seven of the eight **Signals** tracks made the grade (losing out was the elegant and regal, ennui-laden ballad *Losing It*, violin solo and string arrangement courtesy of Ben Mink, who would figure prominently on Geddy's solo album years later).

Support acts on the **Signals** tour included The Jon Butcher Axis, Golden Earring, Heart, Nazareth, the aforementioned Marillion and Payolas, UB40, Vandenberg, White Wolf, Wrabit, Y&T and again Rory Gallagher.

"By that time, we were really trying to develop rear-screen projection stuff," recalls Alex of the tours in the early '80s. "And it was quite a nightmare. Eventually, we had two projectors going, and synching them up was a nightmare — a lot of problems. Staging, of course, changed with every tour. Lighting changed, as the instruments themselves changed, structurally had changed. Also there were the different levels that Howard would use in bringing the audience into it more — using surround sound as well.

"*The Three Stooges* thing we used I think on three different tours, three different occasions," confirms Alex, who goes on to address the subject of Rush's sense of humor. "I think our humor is that goofy, dry sort of humor, typically Canadian; I guess a cross between *Monty Python* and something American. But when we're making a record, whether it's a musical thing or some piece of artwork, or some sort of goofy thing, almost always, in the end, we take a step back and say, 'You know what?

That will be funny now, for the next two weeks, but in five years it's probably not going to be very funny.' So we've always tended to be a little more serious about the presentation and what goes on the record.

"But within the band itself, when we're around each other, honestly, we spend 80% of the time just laughing and goofing around and cutting each other up. Like kids. Because, in a lot of ways, we're just those kids that got together to start this band. I haven't really had to grow up. You know, I hang around with younger people; I mean, I have my whole life. I've never had to be really serious about those kind of life things that so many other people are — to a degree. I take my responsibilities seriously, but you know what I mean [laughs]."

But improving oneself was also always part of the mix. "We would do stuff on the road, just challenge ourselves in another way," says Alex. "On the **Signals** tour, we took the Berlitz French course on the road, and we would have different instructors in every city we went to. We had our books, and we'd sit on the bus and speak French to each other and all of that. And sadly, because you don't use it all the time . . . I'm very rusty with it, I think. We probably all are.

"But, boy, we were doing pretty good. And it's just another way of taking what can be dead time and being a little more constructive with it. I love playing golf. Geddy and I have played tennis for the last 25 years at least on the road. That was the big sport for us. And about ten years ago I started playing golf. So that's really my outlet now on the road. We still do the tennis thing. Geddy loves going to art galleries. We go to movies." Neil, true to his tenacity, stuck with the French lessons for two tours (after all, he did have a house in Quebec), while Alex and Geddy bowed out after one, Geddy's interest somewhat lingering since he had a son taking French immersion in school.

Grace Under Pressure

It's all a blur, an organic gray-scale melding, but indeed, on Grace Under Pressure, one can hear the starting, startling vestiges of the hectic, wiry, steely sound that would become the band's trademark through the rest of the '80s and '90s. Along with Signals, it is one of the Rush records regalvanizing lapsed fans at a quick pace. Less overtly synth-laden than Signals, Grace Under Pressure strikes a balance between guitars and keyboards that rejuvenates the sense of jubilant trioness Rush evoked on remembrances past. There are indeed added tricks — particularly in the percussion area — yet subtler ones, and all told the record's completion was one of the hardest won of the catalog, eclipsing both Hemispheres and Counterparts in the pain-for-gain sweepstakes.

"Well, we changed producers for one thing," explains Alex, "change" not quite capturing the escapade, which included interviewing over 50 candidates. "**Signals** was the last record that Terry Brown did with us; Peter Henderson came in for **Grace**. But he was really on our B-list as a producer. We had planned to work with Steve Lillywhite for that record, but there was some problem at the last moment, and we had to go to our B-list. Because we don't really want to do these things on our own, we like working with a producer. We like having another opinion, and we like having someone who is responsible for another side of the production, and we don't really want to take time to do it when we're actually writing and recording. So Peter came in, but in the long run Peter was a bit of a disappointment. And we ended up working much harder on that record than we ended up anticipating as a band. I think we were in the studio for four and a half months, and we had one day off in that whole time, and that was in the first weekend. So it definitely was a lot of pressure [laughs] to do that record.

"But I agree with you. That was a bit of a sleeper for me for a long time, but I think there's good stuff on it. I like the mood and the sound of that record. I think with **Signals** we had some good songs on there, but I think it suffered in terms of production; it could've been a much better record."

"Steve Lillywhite is really not a man of his word," notes Geddy as he reflects on the making of the album. "After agreeing to do our record, he got an offer from Simple Minds, changed his mind, blew us off and went and did the Simple Minds record. So it put us in a horrible position where we were on the verge of entering preproduction and suddenly we had no producer. All the while we were writing and arranging material we had producers flying in, like every week, to meet with, to talk to. And it was just horrible timing, after going and trying to venture out on our own without our father figure, Terry Brown. It was very disconcerting suddenly to have to go through this whole interview process with somebody else.

"Anyway, at the end of the day, we settled on Peter Henderson, who had a vast amount of engineering and coproducing experience with Supertramp and various artists. And his taste in music was right up our alley, and he seemed like a good guy.

"We went into the studio to start making the record, and we realized that he couldn't make a decision," continues Geddy. "So it was very frustrating because we had to make all the decisions all of a sudden. And it turned out we had literally hired an engineer who was a brilliant engineer. I mean, really, he was one of the best engineers I've ever

worked with. But he was not much help in picking material; he was a very indecisive guy, and that became a nightmare for us. We were in Morin Heights for months making that record, just recording so many tracks, so many different ways for each song, mostly driven by the fact that we really produced the record ourselves, and we were doing it all ourselves. It was a tremendous amount of pressure on ourselves to make the right decisions."

Geddy makes a final summation. "I mean, I like that album, and I just wish I could separate my own personal experience from it, but I can't. It was such an incredibly difficult record for me to make, so I have a hard time separating it out. Although I did some listening to it a couple of months ago, Between the Wheels and that, and I just love them; they're really dense. Peter Henderson was a very good engineer. I do think he did a great job recording the album. Although a producer he's not."

Recording in an unforgiving eastern Canadian setting in the dead of winter, Rush would dress up the experience with Christmas lights, snow-diving, skiing, movies, good food and much liquid merriment, just the salve on the wounds of too much unexpected work. A side trip to Ottawa would find photography's reigning lord, Yousuf Karsh, craft the portrait of the band for the album's back cover.

The resulting record would have a cold — even a cold war — feel to it, a frost reinforced by the elegant but chilling cover art. The band spoke

at the time about all sorts of bad news surround-sounding their lives and times. In the external realm, Neil listed acid rain, the incident of the Korean 747 being shot down, the cruise missile crisis and a healthy quantity of, and quality to, on-going wars. Gloomy, minor-keyed synth tones would drone ominously in agreement, but Alex would be churning in step, adding more riffs per square inch than on the album previous. Indeed, Geddy, a couple of years later, mused that with **Grace** the band had actually swung too far toward the guitars, which smoth-ered the record's melodies, and that the subsequent album, **Power Windows**, had gotten the balance right.

The Body Electric, with its expansive, atmospheric, military drum pattern, would be an odd first single, the song never really catching on in the hearts of fans. Kid Gloves, with its circular riff and 5/4 beat, would be the record's warmest jaunt, **Grace**'s Limelight, Spirit or New World Man, as it were. Yet it's the prog rock reggae pastiche of opener Distant Early Warning that would provide the record with its live-lasting, concert-consummate moment. The track's heavy chorus roils beneath a poignant, straightfor-ward few lyrics, this surging section set up by a rhythmic prechorus that continues to raise the energy bar at many a Rush show. Distant Early Warning would provide the soundtrack for the band's first production video, an appropriately futuristic set and script ensuing.

Elsewhere, Afterimage is an emotional bundle of nervy critical mass, the track eulogizing the life of Robbie Whelan, assistant to engineer Paul Northfield. Says Geddy, "Afterimage was a very personal song and was really about the loss of a friend. So I think we took extra care with that song to make sure it was very heartfelt and that recording went well."

Both reggae and other things co-opted by The Police are co-opted yet again by Rush — and probably more so than on any previous album — most pertinently by the man behind the kit, for Red Sector A, The Enemy Within, Red Lenses and Between the Wheels. It is a thread that is there, yet it is a complicated tangle of influence that is internalized, mastered and personalized by the band.

"Yes, I think there was an influence," agrees Geddy. "I remember Pratt was always having Marley or somebody on in the bus. In those days,

when we all traveled by bus, of course, our musical tastes influenced each other, because everybody had to take turns to put on the records they wanted while you're driving and driving and driving. So there was always music playing; we were always talking about music, and I think that was one of the great benefits of that kind of travel as a band. You've always got something on the box, and you're always talking about it. So the whole life of music never ends. You finish the gig, and you're on your way, but you're listening and talking, 'I like this; I don't like that,' so you have constant input.

"And I think in later days it's harder to have that atmosphere, because you spend much more time individually on your own. So you don't share those things until you get into a writing environment or a control room environment or something like that. You still might talk about those things in the dressing room and say, 'Hey, check this record out' or 'Check that record out.' That often happens.

"I guess if you listen to **Permanent Waves**, you know, you can hear little bits of reggae, such as that little bit on *Spirit of Radio*. **Signals** was probably the first one. Songs like *New World Man*, even *Vital Signs* to a certain degree, are starting to show a different influence rhythmically. I think they were the signs that we needed to . . . that we couldn't just play rock. We needed to listen to other stuff, and we needed to see if there was

any place for that other stuff in our songs. And it probably began with **Signals**, I think. And from there you can kind of pinpoint different experiments. I mean, some of them were failed experiments, but that doesn't matter. Some were successful, some weren't. *New World Man* was very influenced by that whole ska thing. Actually, it was more ska than even reggae, to a certain degree. At the time, we were in England a lot, and those ska bands were on the radio at the time. They had infectious rhythms, so, yes, they had an influence on us."

As a final **Grace** note, *The Enemy Within* is Part 1 of Neil's *Fear* trilogy, presented in reverse order, Part 2 being *The Weapon* from **Signals**, Part 3 being *Witch Hunt* from **Moving Pictures**. Reflecting one of the many philosophies rifling through the well-read Peart, responsibility and response begin and end with the individual.

Touring for the album took Rush to all four corners of America from May 8th through July 12th of '84, the band then hitting Quebec for three shows in mid-July before a six-week summer vacation. On September 14th, it was back into the eastern States (along with two pink- and gold-lit dates at home for a video-documented Maple Leaf Gardens stand), the rustbelt and the south through November 9th, and then off to Japan for the first time for four dates in mid-November, followed by a two-night stand in Honolulu on the way home. Two shows were postponed due to illness, and these were quite remarkably made up only days later. Oddly, both pairings were dates in New Haven, Connecticut.

Surprise selections for the tour included *Witch Hunt* from **Moving Pictures**, played live for the first time (capping the *Fear* trilogy suite in its entirety), along with *Finding My Way* hauled back into focus, albeit in medley form. Every track from the **Grace Under Pressure** album was

played on tour, with two garnering only part-time status, *Afterimage* being replaced by *Kid Gloves* in September. Support on the tour came from the likes of Fastway, Helix, Gary Moore, Red Rider (at the Maple Leaf Gardens shows), Strict-Neine (the two Hawaiian shows), The Tenants and Pat Travers.

"We almost always want to play too many of the new songs, more than will fit," says Neil, underscoring that obvious fact, in stark contrast to the average live set list, where bands might pepper three, maybe four, tracks in among the time-honored but intellectually lax phenomenon of jukeboxing. "It's always a question of whittling down which ones are more enjoyable and more successful live. Because there is certainly a difference between a good recording song and a good performance song. But generally it is a juggling act, increasingly difficult to get in all the old stuff, because, unlike most bands, we don't really hate our old stuff. A lot of it is still really challenging and enjoyable to play. I've said it before — *Tom Sawyer* I can play every night for the rest of my life, and it'll never get easy [laughs]. And a lot of our older songs are not just fun to play but satisfying to get right. That's the thing that keeps you interested every night, which is always challenging."

"Yeah, I loved Pat's style of playing," reflects Alex on one of the more regular backups on the tour, fellow Canadian Pat Travers. "It's a really blues-based style of playing, but he was a superconfident guy, to the point of being cocky. But I was really impressed. You know, I've always been — not so much in the last so many years — but I used to be very self-conscious and a little lacking in self-confidence. When I watched guys like him, it was like, oh, I wish I just had that, the balls to just . . . bleaagh, go for it [tossing his arms open]. And I didn't always feel like that about my guitar playing specifically. I always felt there was so much more to improve on. Yeah, I'd go and watch him, and we got along really, really well with the whole band — Tommy Aldridge, great drummer. He and Neil got on really well. He was a lot of fun to be with."

"That was one of the nice things we liked about having an opening act," seconds Neil. "We always liked to have a good opening act, and we got things off to a high standard. And certainly I liked having good drummers to work with, which we often did. Tommy Aldridge, wonderful drummer. I always liked watching him, and again having that

caliber of band on the same show was much nicer than having a not good one [laughs]. We had Rod Morgenstein with the Steve Morse Band on one tour. In the early days, there was Gary McCracken with Max Webster, Marty Deller with FM, and later on Herb with Primus."

"We had a terrible situation in Japan once," notes Geddy, when asked about memorable experiences on the tour. "After our show, I think we had a day off in Osaka, and we had done the traditional Japanese bathhouse and massage. We were very relaxed, and we were sitting in the hotel bar having a few drinks with our road crew, and we heard some terrible shouting, and Neil was ensconced in this argument with this Japanese man who was insisting on beating his wife in public. And Neil, of course, was trying to get him to cool down. And the harder he tried to get him to cool down, the harder he was hitting his wife. And of course we all came out there full of whiskey and anger and tried to break it up. But the hotel security staff was treating us like we were wrong, like we were interfering in a personal squabble, to the point where we were being carted away. I guess apparently this Japanese fellow was a Yakuza member or something. Anyway, they did not appreciate us trying to help the woman, who ended up, when last we saw her, she was laid out on the floor. It was pretty ugly."

"Actually, we only went once, and I don't think we slept the whole time there," laughs Alex when asked for his impressions of the place. "It was only four dates. It was so unique; the audience was unlike anything we'd ever played for, so programmed. They all jumped up and clapped at the same time like crazy, then sat down and didn't move. When they left the venue, there was not a shred of paper or anything on the floor, extremely neat. They have that light system at the Budokan; it's like a streetlight, where if it's green you can have fun and cheer, if it's amber sit down in your seat. If it's red, the concert stops, and everybody goes home. And they would stand up in groups. You would have six people stand up and cheer and go crazy; they would all be wearing orange sweatshirts. Then this group over here with green sweatshirts would stand up and cheer, then sit down. It was the most bizarre thing.

"And then Hawaii, Hawaii was a riot [laughs]. We had such a great time. It was just an extension of the whole crazy tour. We got there, and I think we had a couple of days off, and then we had the show there. My recognition of it is that it was just like any American show."

Power Windows

"That's one I particularly really like," pipes Neil Peart, with respect to Rush's album for 1985, Power Windows. Indeed, Geddy goes further and calls the album his favorite of the entire '80s and '90s, followed by Roll the Bones and Test for Echo.

In much the same manner that he visualizes A Farewell to Kings and Hemispheres as a duo, Peart looks at Power Windows and Hold Your Fire as forming a synergistic pairing. "If you try to divorce yourself from musician to fan, I think as a fan I would particularly like those records, just because they are such a feast to listen to — so much texture and so much variety and rhythmic exploration. To me, they remain very satisfying pieces of work to listen to. So I think that's about the highest tribute I can give it: they are something that I would like as a fan."

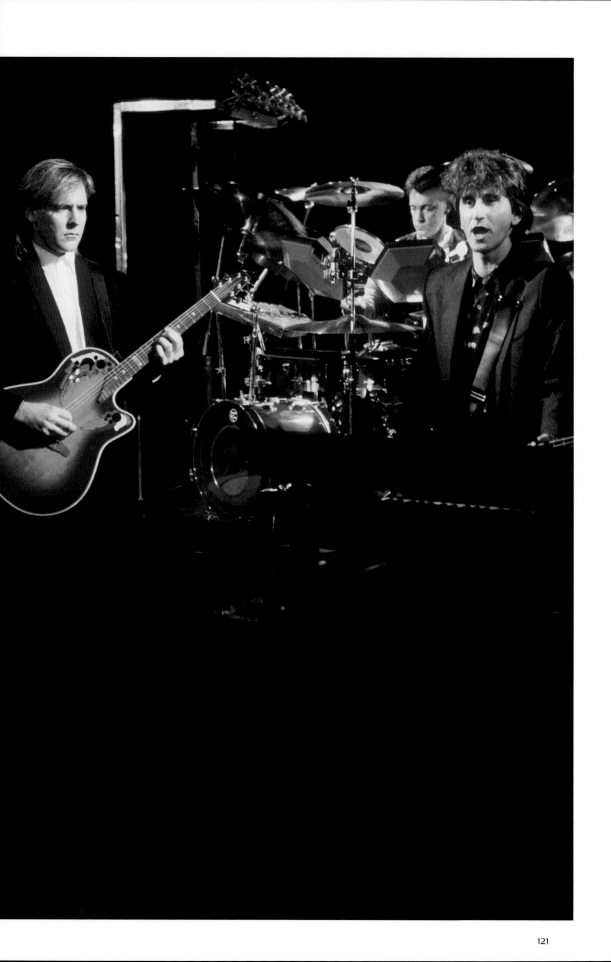

Prompted to contrast the two as much as possible, Neil opines that "**Hold Your Fire** is somehow a little more introvert in mood, musically and lyrically, as much as they tend to feed on each other. That definitely strikes me now, just thinking about it. **Power Windows** is more dynamic and more extrovert, while **Hold Your Fire** is more textural and introvert, both lyrically and musically. But I like them equally in their two moods. **Power Windows** really hangs together well as a whole body of work, I think, the way it's shaped. Running order is something we've always spent a lot of time and debate on. And I think it's a great running order on this; from top to bottom, I think it's a really good performance. Nope, I like that one."

Fan reaction was particularly guarded, many finding the album too high-tech, too glossy, not guitar-crunched enough. Indeed, **Power Windows** was spiced liberally with electronics from both Geddy (synths inextricably linked to the '80s) and Neil, with his percussion samples. Neil concurs. "Those two albums were very much embroiled in all that. We were working with Peter Collins, who was equally ambitious as a producer and arranger and song designer in a lot of ways. And we were working with a keyboard player, Andy Richards [Strawbs, Trevor Horn, Frankie Goes to Hollywood, Propaganda], in England at that time who was king of the flourishes and the dramatic moments and all of that."

I asked Neil about the significance of the title and cover art. "It just came about. In those days, I would just be writing a group of songs without a particular idea or concept in mind. And very often, as with both **Power Windows** and with **Hold Your Fire**, a common thread emerged through the course of the writing, and I realized, of course, the common denominator here was power, different kinds of power. So it was a tongue-in-cheek kind of idea, power windows, looking out at power, simple as that. And then Hugh Syme, the art director, always has a quirky sense of humor, as with **Moving Pictures**, always wanting to twist it in a couple of more directions if he can."

Unsurprisingly, Peter Henderson would not be in the production chair again. Enter Peter Collins, summed up this way by Neil when asked to contrast his vibe with that of the band's producer, Terry Brown. "It's not really quantifiable because we were a different band, and to stop work with someone like Terry Brown wasn't a reflection on him or our relationship with him. It's just that you share a certain period of time and growth, and then we were restless for difference. It's not a question of better or superior ability or anything. So Peter Collins came along, again, when we were much more interested in song arrangement and all that, which is absolutely his forte. So he contributed to that element of our growth and was very great to work with as a friend. But Terry Brown was too; for that period, we were very close, and he has a great personality and character in the studio. There's no comparison in any terms of good or bad. It's simply the people we were at the time. Like any relationship, I guess."

Peter came heartily recommended by Thin Lizzy's Gary Moore, who had been a Rush backup act. Other than that, said Geddy at the time, Peter's credits, such as Musical Youth and Nik Kershaw, were quite obviously non-Rush-like. Add Blancmange and Tracey Ullman to that, and the connection gets no clearer, which is the way Geddy wanted it. Why not have someone in who knew things the band didn't know?

Conversely, why bother with someone who was primarily versed in skills the three had already brought to the room?

The star track on **Power Windows** would be the expansive yet immediate *The Big Money*, released as a single in October of '85, one month before the album's debut. Indicative of those electric and eclectic '80s percussion sounds and cutting synthesizer tones, the song is in fact a tour de force of arrangement, mood, movements and emotional ebbs and flows, quite a handful for the radio hit it was. *Manhattan Project* was another strong track, one that mirrored *Distant Early Warning* in nuclear pursuit as well as lay-low riff, building prechorus and then explosive, rock-out chorus. At the time, Neil spoke of the paring process, of distilling a dozen books of nuclear history down to a hundred words of atomic accuracy. The outcome was a song that didn't address the obvious, focusing more on the extraordinary minds behind the weaponry.

Much of the midriff of the album is highly textural, the songs being colorized by an obtuse guitar, a coterie of traditional and futuristic production instruments, constant, dependable bass and songs that creep around and only pay back (the proverbial money shot, as it were) come chorus time. *Middletown Dreams* finds Neil revisiting *Subdivisions* terrain, referencing the escape into an irresistible embrace with a powerfully seductive muse so apocryphally experienced by both Sherwood Anderson and Paul Gauguin as well as any musician — pick one — even Peart himself. Finishing strongly, **Power Windows** offers the stirring *Emotion Detector* and finally *Mystic Rhythms*, which seems to sum up the collective mindspace of neoprog positors and those of old proggers renewed such as Yes, Genesis and Peter Gabriel, the track lunging forward into six minutes of eastern exotics. About the lyric, Neil professes a curiosity about things unseen. Yet, ultimately, he holds back, straddling the line between believing and tending toward belief.

Recording **Power Windows** was not a cheap affair. Venues such as Richard Branson's The Manor and Air Studios on Montserrat were utilized, as was Abbey Road Studios. Then there's the matter of a 30-piece orchestra on three tracks and a 25-person choir, used for the angelic closing sublimity of *Marathon*.

"Parts of that record we recorded at Abbey Road Studios, which was a huge thrill for us," says Geddy. "A lot of the orchestra were London Symphony players, and it was the big room in Abbey Road where so many big records had been recorded; that was the first time we used an orchestra in any of our songs, I believe, so that was a real treat. We all arrived at Abbey Road, and we were all like kids again, going through this famous place and sitting in that magnificent room. Of course, it was

terribly disconcerting to see all these symphonic musicians, and in between takes they're fucking around, cutting things up [laughs]. We're overhearing all these disparaging, typical comments. You know, you have this impression of symphonic musicians, and then you realize they're just musicians like us [laughs].

"But it was really a lot of fun. I was walking around taking photos, and it was a pretty cool moment. At the same time, we recorded a choir for *Marathon*, and then we went to this church in another part of London where this really marvelous choir was singing, and it was a really great sounding room, and that's why Peter wanted to record them in that room.

"Having been in a three-piece band who worked only with each other for so many years, it was gratifying to work with Peter, to suddenly start going to these really interesting nooks and crannies of London and working with these other musicians and other arrangers. We worked with Anne Dudley on that record, a wonderful arranger. She used to be in Art of Noise and had worked a lot with Trevor Horn. It was a great experience to suddenly realize that there's all these other talented people out there who can contribute to your music and yet not take away from it, just enhance it. It was a real awakening, in terms of production and arrangement and as musicians."

The **Power Windows** tour was preceded by the 1985 spring training tour, which saw the band play five dates in Florida, indulging Geddy's love of baseball. *Middletown Dreams* and *The Big Money* were previewed at this time in early form, while other tracks from the album were fleshed out during soundchecks. "I remember *Big Money* really improved after that," recalls Geddy with respect to spring training. "We got the right kind of rock-out attitude in certain parts of the song; when we played it, certain parts of the song got an instant cheer. And that kind of thing is a great confidence builder."

The tour proper started up six months later on December 4th, the band once more beginning with America, virtually in its entirety, before interspersing a few central Canadian and western Canadian dates into the mix. Seven of the **Power Windows** tracks would make the live grade, either for the whole tour or for part of it, with *Grand Designs* offered in medley form, segueing into the effortlessly crowd-pleasing *In the Mood*. Only *Emotion Detector* wouldn't be played.

Belying their tradition of gathering quality musicians for support acts, Rush called upon The Steve Morse Band, FM, Marillion, Fabulous Thunderbirds and old tourmates Blue Öyster Cult to fill the bill. Saskatchewan metal upstarts Kick Axe appropriately jumped on for the short western Canadian stint. "He's so great," said Alex of Steve Morse, now, of course, part of Deep Purple. "He backed us up on a couple tours. There's another one where I just went out and watched him every night; he was so good, such a great all-around player." Indeed, contact with Morse was made during the spring training tour, pilot Steve being a Florida native who, Ian Gillan told me recently, lives on an airstrip with four planes and his home studio.

"My first relation to it is what kind of drum set did I have?" says Neil, trying to dredge up some memories of the **Power Windows** tour. "And I remember, yeah, that was the kind of pinkie Ludwig ones [laughs]; that's an important touchstone. And of course we were embroiled in a lot of music technology at that time. So the live performance was . . . talk about a challenge, a real undertaking, in coordinating it. We were still trying to juggle expanding our sound so much with Geddy taking on so many keyboards and both of them triggering so many keyboard events with feet and hands and all of that. And I was getting much into sampling at that time too, so that was a time of particular ferment and experimentation in technological ways.

"The performance live, it reflected . . . when The Who first started performing **Who's Next**, and Keith Moon had to play the tapes of *Baba O'Riley* and *Won't Get Fooled Again*, and they were trying to work at the forefront of technology at the time, it was difficult and frustrating, and **Quadrophenia** was largely sabotaged by trying to do too much with tapes and all that. That's in the '70s. Go ten years later, when sampling and midi became available. Because it's available, of course, we wanted to

use it [laughs]. It made possible so much. But in the context of live performance particularly, then we became nervously dependent on a lot of technology, where we would have to hear certain sequences and triggering going on to stay in synch with each other."

Neil knew the album was going to be a difficult one to get across profoundly in the acoustic crudity of hockey barns, but the challenge had to be met. "We had to reproduce that," he explains. "I guess that's part of the personal onus for us. We really felt the challenge of wanting to reproduce what was on the record. Yes, we could have played just a stripped-down version of anything, as we could now, but for me using sampling is a good example. I always like to use things that I could physically play. So every sound was the result of a hit or kick; there was an organic relationship there that to me was kind of a point of honor. So those were the kinds of issues we were balancing at that time.

"So, yeah, those two records, those two tours, I think represent the apogee of that particular involvement in music and arranging. We were very ambitious as arrangers then. I was describing before how the course of study becomes your learning. You begin to play first, and then you learn how to write songs, then you're trying to learn how to arrange them and produce them. And that is the course of study that I think almost goes that linear. For our band anyway. We started off certainly concentrating on playing, and then it became that progress of wanting to refine skills. So that period also coincided with all of that.

"Technology became more reliable — that's the thing. God, when we first started with sequencers in the early '80s, they were so unreliable. **Signals** and, well, even **Moving Pictures** had *Vital Signs* on it, which was sequencer-based. So that was something I had to hear on stage every night to be able to play to. And then into **Signals** and **Grace Under Pressure**, it was experimenting with all the early synthesizer advances and all the attendant frustrations and unreliability. Now that stuff is unbelievable, how reliable it is night after night. The last two tours, that stuff just works [laughs]. So it's really different now."

In talking about the evolution of the drum solo throughout the years and into the '80s, its relationship to the technology surrounding it (sound and vision), Neil explains that the entire spectacle is predicated from his roost. "I trigger everything that happens. Yeah, everything that happens in the drum solo is me — all the sounds, the movies, I don't play that — it plays to me [laughs]. It's true, though, in the early '80s, I started adding more electronic stuff. I remember I first had the 360 degree drum set for **Grace Under Pressure**, which allowed me to use the Simmons drums and stuff. And that grew as sampling came along. That was so irresistible to me to have every percussion sound in the universe under my sticks and feet. Then I would have the pads and foot triggers and the midi keyboard percussion. It was a great thing for me to be able to have glockenspiel, tubular bells, marimba, all that, right beside me. So all of those just became liberating devices, more than restrictive. Likewise when I had the drum set going around, there's all those noises, I'm triggering all of those sounds, on the marimba as it goes, and, yeah, the film and all that, I'm not synched to them, they try to synch to me. So again that's all driven by me."

So there is an external person changing the film? "Oh, I have nothing to do with it. I just play," laughs Neil. "And because editing rhythm is loose enough, it seems to fall right on the tempo, even when it's not."

It is of note that there was no European tour for **Power Windows**. "Well, we didn't tour Europe every time," says Neil. "It's been ten years now since we've been there and longer in between. That's the easy answer, simple supply and demand. There's always more demand for us to play places than supply of us wanting to do it [laughs]."

"That was a gradual thing, a hard-learned lesson," adds Geddy on the subject of Rush reducing their touring commitments. "You only learn those things when your life is falling apart and you realize you've just spent too much time away. And I would say from '85 on we started learning those lessons and slowly started pulling back our touring dates. That's when we stopped playing outside of America so much. After the Japanese tour, we just started pulling back the reins, cutting our American tour dates, making sure we instituted a policy where, if we were out for three weeks, we would come home for ten days afterwards. We started playing less American cities; we stopped playing Europe every tour. We would play every other tour or three tours, and eventually we just ignored Europe completely.

"So that was the beginning. We just all made a more concerted effort to take time away from the band and pay attention to our families and kids and all that stuff. At that point, we were still traveling by bus, which

. . . you can get the nicest bus in the world, but it's still a bus, and it's very hard on your system to do the gig, get on the bus, drive for 400 miles and get up in the middle of the night and go into your hotel room and finish sleeping. And it lends itself to a lot of abuse, because you're so bored on the damn bus. You drink more than you should, you smoke more than you should, all that stuff. It's a tough environment, and I think it's one that contributes to a lot of physical deterioration."

I asked Geddy if there was something in particular about the Japanese experience that made the band not go back. "Well, there was the incident in the hotel, but it's not that that put us off going to Japan. I think it put Neil off of going back to Japan in a big hurry. But it was just a coincidental thing with us going to Europe, going to Japan. It looked like, if we let this thing keep going, there were any number of countries we could expand to. And it's like, 'Do we have the time, can we afford this in our lives, to be a band 12 months a year?' And we didn't. We realized we couldn't do that. So that's when we said, 'Look, we're not here to dominate the world. We are thankful we've had this much success. Let's just step back a bit, take stock of our lives at this point and try to bring some reasonable attitude to living.'"

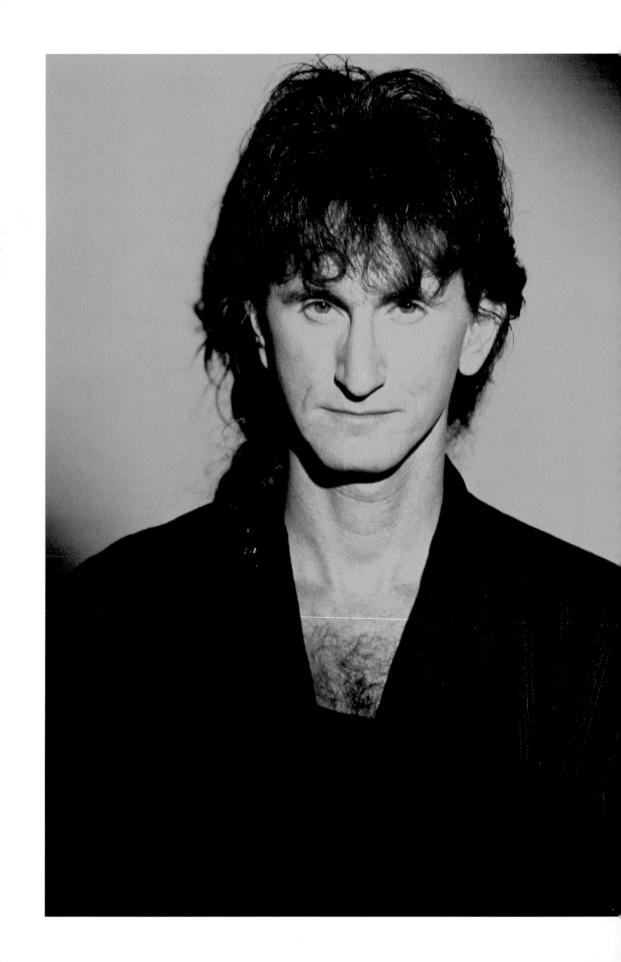

Hold Your Fire

"I think all of these were done pretty much in the same pattern," says Neil of the Power Windows, Hold Your Fire, Presto era of the band. "We would go off to the country and do the songwriting and get the rough forms of the songs worked out and make demos and make preproduction with the producer, go into the studio and record basic tracks, do the overdubs and then the mixing. Although we might have moved from studio to studio with different ones, that was definitely the mode of work we had evolved through that period, and we didn't change really until Vapor Trails which we recorded and wrote in a whole other way. At that point, we had the luxury of choosing and allocating our time. It really was at the time of Permanent Waves, I guess, when we started being able to do that, going away together and working on the material and going into the studio. Through this time, we eventually gathered more luxury for increased time in different studios and all that. But basically the method evolved back then. That was the first time we went away to work on an album before we recorded it."

"**Hold Your Fire** was a good record," adds Alex. "We were sort of coming to the end of our foray into the world of keyboards. **Power Windows** was so layered with keyboards, and **Hold Your Fire** was a bit of a relief; we kind of pulled back a little bit on the use of keyboards. But it was part of the '80s thing; that was the sort of headspace we were at then." On the subject of that headspace, Alex takes a break to have a chuckle over press shots of the band back then, pointing out the bright new wave outfits, pageboy haircuts, Geddy's big glasses, stopping at one of many live shots of himself in various *Miami Vice* suits and tuxes, offering, "Yeah, and right after this I ask the crowd, 'May I take your order?'"

Geddy remarks about how shocked he was at how good **Hold Your Fire** is after all these years, calling it one of the band's "dark horses," adding that "it's a very ambitious piece, full of textural changes, dramatic, rhythmic changes. And it's quite a romantic album in some ways, melodically. The song *Mission* is really a song I'm proud of in terms of melody and a kind of boldness, taking it in the direction we did. That record was influenced a lot by Peter Collins in the sense that his love of melody and what we'd gone through on **Power Windows** was still resonating with us. Some of those were very, very difficult songs to put together, texturally.

"I remember *Mission* was a song Peter Collins just loved. And at some point in Britain, when we were working on it, he really wanted to do what he called The Full Monty — put orchestra and choir on it . . . and there's a particular sound of an English brass band, which I guess was something he grew up with that we had no feel for, the kind of band you saw in the park on Sunday playing the gazebo. He was kind of obsessed with finding an authentic one. And he tracked one down in the north of

England, and he wanted them to play on this track. We were really working hard on that record, and there was this weekend where this band was available. We were all supposed to fly up there to record them, and we just said, 'Look, Pete, you go. You know what you want, we're pooped, why don't you go and record them? This will be a treat for you.' And he did. And he brought it back, and he was all excited about it of course. And we never really shared the same enthusiasm for it [laughs]. And, in the end, the version of the song that we released was kind of stripped down; I don't think we used the brass band very much. We didn't use the whole arrangement. So there is another version of that song that exists that I hope we'll release that has The Full Monty on it."

One might argue that the record is stuffed with Full Montys. Like **Power Windows**, a menagerie of expensive locations was patronized and swanned through. The Manor, Ridge Farm, Air Studios in Montserrat, locations back home in Ontario, mixing hotspots in Paris, a seat for strings, one up north for Peter's oompa band, mastering in Maine . . . the end result was an album similar in technological icings to **Power Windows** with some quietly classic Rush-worthy accomplishments.

Opener *Force Ten* is a brisk, tough one, ironically the last song written for the album (and with cowboy hats on, says Geddy), as per the band's tradition of conjuring up a quickly conceived afterthought, this one penned in three hours. Max Webster lyricist Pye Dubois returns for another word wrestle with Peart. *Time Stand Still* is a master of melodics, distinguished by an ethereal Aimee Mann come chorus time. Launched as a single, the song didn't fare all that well in the States, although the UK still professed its love, sending it to #42 in the charts.

The album closes on an Oriental note, with *Turn the Page* containing Buddhist references, *Tai Shan* documenting Peart's Chinese climbing expedition and *High Water* marrying Peart's comfort with, and through, water to a similar sentiment within the psyche of the Japanese. The last two go there musically as well. It all added up to a meticulous mélange of complicated, progressive, perky, percussive pop, eye to the future or at minimum the right now.

Alex agrees that these late '80s records took on a much different tone than those quickly crafted in the unadulterated power trio days. "They certainly did. From a guitar standpoint, my sound had really changed. It was much more wiry and brighter. Part of the reason for that is, again, there was such a conflict between all the keyboards stuff that was happening and where the guitar fit into that. The main part of the problem is, when we made those records, we decided to do all the keyboards

stuff before we did the guitar stuff. And it was just a scheduling thing more than anything. It was just more convenient to do the keyboards that way. When it came time to do guitars, it was hard to figure out where the guitar was going to fit in because there was so much of this going on. And I think with **Hold Your Fire** we kind of reached a peak, and that was it. And then every album after that we just gradually started to thin out the keyboards."

Neil agrees with Alex's description of the guitar sound as "wiry" but

with an asterisk. "Yeah, but that was his choice of the guitars and the guitar sound he was going for at the time, you know? No one to blame for it. And if you listen to other music from the time, there was a prevalent guitar sound. The Fixx and stuff was highly compressed. Processed, I call it — processed guitar sounds. That's what he wanted! You know, hindsight is a pretty useless thing [laughs]. Drumming-wise, I always just wanted a great natural drum sound, with the addition of all the electronic effects and stuff. But that's been the linear pursuit for me, just getting a really great natural drum sound."

Six of the album's ten tracks would make the live set, with *Open Secrets*, *Second Nature*, *Tai Shan* and *High Water* remaining etched-in-time recorded relics only. The tour was a six-month affair that straddled 1988. The band made it back to eastern Canada for what was only the third time ever, the first in a dozen years, the first time ever all the way to Newfoundland, where the jaunt kicked off.

Peart looks back on the situation. "It was because we were getting so much flack from the east coast about not going there. There was a big petition out from a Halifax radio station, thousands of people signing this petition. And I saw them on MuchMusic at the time, lodging this protest. And so I thought, 'OK, OK! You know, we're not trying to insult anyone; we'll go there!'"

After eastern Canada, it was back into well-mined, very familiar terrain, including all of America, the populous bits of Ontario and Quebec, the obligatory three large western Canadian cities and then the

usual good coverage of the UK, closing off in Rotterdam and two stops in Germany come early May of '88. Support included Chalk Circle, The Rainmakers, Michael Schenker Group, Tommy Shaw and, in Germany, Wishbone Ash.

"Our productions got incredibly complicated at that point," explains Geddy, charting the intensification of the band's reliance on technology, beginning with **Grace Under Pressure**, peaking with **Hold Your Fire**. "It was the beginning of the nightmare years for me. We started bringing in banks of samplers and sequencers to try to reproduce all these things that we had now put on our records. So you take a record where maybe the biggest difference was that there was an extra guitar in a song or a little bit of keyboard here and there, and now we had orchestras and choirs. And how do you go on stage and reproduce that? Play that song suddenly without the orchestra and choir? So we had to figure out a way to do all that. And the only way to do that was to bring in these sequencers and samplers. And at that point, they weren't like they are now. Now you can hold down a cluster of keys, and you can play the whole fucking song; it goes forever. In those days, there was only a certain amount of sample time you had per piece. And also, to avoid having to play to a click track and just automate the whole thing . . . we didn't want to do that; we wanted it to be performance-based. So we would have these sequences assigned for each note or each chord part of the song, and, in order to play them live and still play them as a band would play them, I would have to play them in time. So that meant playing bass pedals to keep the

bottom end still there, not playing bass in a particular part of the song and triggering either the chord pattern or the sequence, whatever it was. And in a lot of those songs, there were layers, so you're playing a string part, and you're adding a little accent on the other hand. It was very complex and required a lot of technology and required us to have somebody off stage loading a separate bank of sequencers and samplers for each song.

"And we had to design a failsafe too. What happens if the sampler goes out? It's electronic technology; it's very buggy. At that stage, computer technology also was very buggy. So we designed this whole system that was literally duplicated. Every song was loaded twice, and we had this giant switch that, if one bank of sequencers went down, Tony Geranios, who does my keyboards, could hit this switch, and instantly it would switch to the other bank of samplers.

"And some of it was just too much for me to handle, so we would split some off to Alex, and he would trigger some stuff. And then we'd split some off even to Neil, because he was using electronic drums, although he had his own sampling nightmare going on back there. But sometimes if we had an extra sample that none of us could trigger, we'd give it to him, and he'd stick it on his [laughs]. So we became really trapped in this complex arrangement of keyboards."

With a quick check of the memory, Alex figures that, of all the albums, tracks from **Hold Your Fire** and **Power Windows** are among the least revisited over the course of recent tours. And with reason. "They're so demanding to play live; it's a real workout. And I don't know if you really feel a great sense of satisfaction. I mean, I like listening to those records. They sound really interesting in the whole perspective of all our music. But to play them live, they're so demanding, and you're so stuck in a position by the keyboards and the pedals, it becomes almost a mechanical, mathematical exercise. And they probably get passed over more than anything else. I think **Presto** is another one that doesn't get a lot of play, although we did a lot of the record when we first toured it."

All in all, for Alex, memories of the **Hold Your Fire** tour were not fond: he got the flu, Geddy constantly had a sore throat, and the tour was

long by Rush standards. Emphasizing that there was no talk of breakup, the band *did* consider tossing in the touring towel. Instead, after the longest break the band ever had — seven months, the previous longest being three months — it was back to business as usual.

A Show of Hands

Recordings of the Birmingham, England, shows, along with New Orleans, San Diego and Phoenix dates, all from the Hold Your Fire tour, would be culled with an eye to releasing what would be the band's third live album, A Show of Hands, and the accompanying platinum-selling video of the same name and artwork. Two songs on the record, *Mystic Rhythms* and *Witch Hunt*, would be captured from the preceding Power Windows tour, specifically from a date at The Meadowlands in New Jersey.

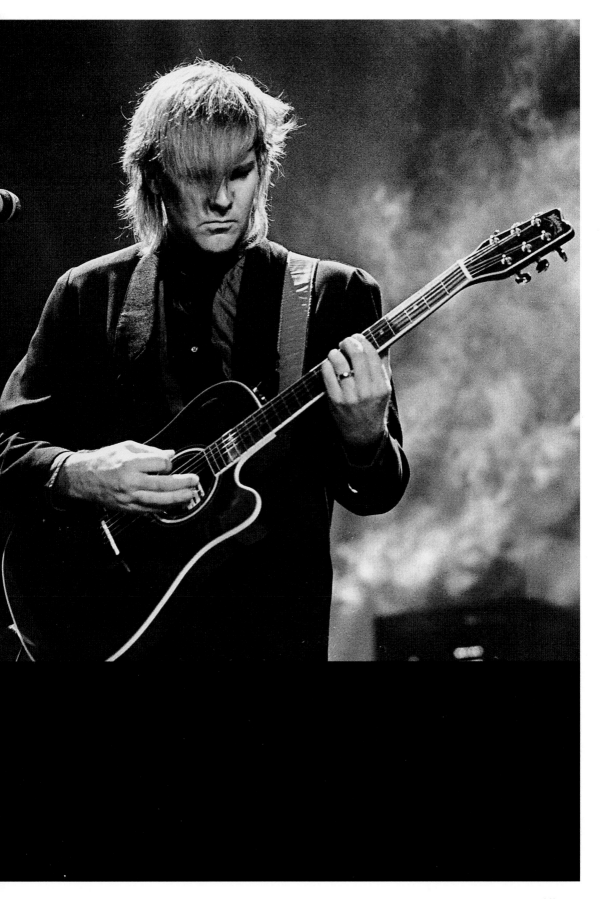

The video version of **A Show of Hands** would include a number of selections not on the double LP album or single CD, namely *Prime Mover, Territories, The Spirit of Radio, Tom Sawyer* and the *2112/La Villa Strangiato/In the Mood* medley used as an encore. *Lock and Key* showed up on first pressings of the US-issued laserdisc.

"**A Show of Hands** to me is a very fine album," says Geddy. "That style of recording a live album, basically taking a handful of shows and choosing the best you've got . . . to me that is a very good representation of that kind of live album. In terms of the construction of it, I think it was down to Paul Northfield and myself mostly."

One can hear the band's cartoony intro music (including, jocularly, *Three Blind Mice*) before the vista-wide entrance of *The Big Money*, which closes in less grand fashion, namely the heavy metal riff from Cheech & Chong's *Earache My Eye*. Offering value for the money, the album contained only two pre-**Signals** selections, *Closer to the Heart* (included due to its explosive climactic finish) and *Witch Hunt*, the latter occurring on a live album for the first time. Neil's drum solo, which had begun going by the name *The Rhythm Method* on the **Hold Your Fire** tour, was not supposed to fit but did after all, even if it is presented in abbreviated form, edits decided by Peart himself.

Presto

For the third time, Rush closed out an era with the release of a live album. Also signifying the transition this time, the band called upon a new producer, Rupert Hine, producer on smash records by Howard Jones, Tina Turner, the Thompson Twins, Stevie Nicks and Power Station. Indeed, Peter Collins had declined to work with the band this time, citing a desire to branch out. The end result would be a record with various gestures toward sonic clarity, from Peart's tight snare sound, to his timid bass and tom tones, to Geddy's deliberate bass-as-lead mids (bravely at the expense of bottom end), to Alex's rainy electric, acoustic and enigmatically semi-acoustic effects, to a totality comprising fewer synths, thinner synths, more bright electric piano and more spaces thereof.

Presto's soar-away highlight is *The Pass*, an encouraging antisuicide number, considerably researched by Peart, which, despite being about *teen* suicide, might be viewed as a cautionary tale to a *Tom Sawyer*-type character with his spark for defiance waning, resulting in a late-in-life epiphany. "*The Pass* is one of the best songs we've ever written," agrees Geddy, who has proven the band's appreciation for it by featuring it on the **Vapor Trails** tour. "I just love that song. There's just something about the atmosphere and the nature of the lyric; it's some of Neil's best writing, and I still think it holds true. I think it deals with a really difficult issue in a very positive way. That song has stayed with me. I love playing it, I love singing it, and I think it's just one of those accomplishments, as a writer. You know, fans view us much differently than we do. They look at us as a band of players, to a large degree. But from the inside looking out, the victories that I look back on usually are when I had a breakthrough as a writer or when I was able to approach something from an arrangement point of view that was new for me. And that's one of those songs."

Deeper into the record, *Anagram* is stuffed with them — it is a word game set to a power pop soundtrack — while *Scars* is full of drums, Neil spending a day constructing a system to play this demanding song that sounds rife with overdubs but isn't. *Superconductor* would be a minor hit, its brisk but airy construction demonstrating that Rush would rock out only on their own terms, despite 1989 being smack in the middle of a huge few years for a harder form of rock. Opener *Show Don't Tell* has turned

out, years later, to be one of the band's most memorable rhythmic labyrinths, swooping rises and precipitous drops exposing Rush's continuous vitality with the '90s around the corner.

"Those were interesting songs, but in retrospect I don't think they're great songs," offers Geddy candidly. "I mean, they're not songs that I look back and say, 'This is our best work.' I don't think so. *The Pass* stands out on that record, and I can't think of any other titles off the top of my head. *Red Tide* is an interesting song. I think they were interesting songs, but I don't think they were profound in terms of writing. I think it's a decent-sounding record, but I think on **Roll the Bones** the writing was far superior. Although I don't think **Roll the Bones** is our best-sounding record, in terms of sonic production."

But, alas, **Presto** is a record out on a limb, somewhat forgotten in admiring scans of the catalog. "I think the other guys have gone on record as saying it's one they really wished they could redo," affirms Neil. "Of course, there are so many elements that come together in a record, the composition, the instrumentation, the sound, orchestration, producer, all of that. And **Presto**'s one that strikes me too; it didn't live up to its own potential even, never mind our potential. Or the potential that was in the material there, for whatever reason. That's what we feel.

But it's pointless to say that because someone who likes that record would go 'What are you saying?! What do you mean blah, blah, blah?!' That's a lesson we learned long ago. Don't dare to criticize even your own work because somebody's going to take you to task for it. OK, you know best!"

"Let me remember that record for a moment," laughs Geddy when prompted for his impression. "**Presto** is the first record we did with Rupert Hine and Stevie Tayler [Rupert's engineer, dubbed rookie of the year for his volleyball skills at the venerable Morin Heights pitch]. So that was a slight departure for us in writing style and also in production team, having just come out of a couple records with Peter Collins, which was a great experience for us, where we worked in England a lot. And I think with Rupert we were more determined to try to work closer to home. He came over, and we did some writing at a farmhouse near Toronto. Stylistically, we were experimenting more with songwriting, experimenting in different songwriting techniques, which is why we wanted to work with Rupert. He had worked with good songwriters in the past and was a musician himself. His input was very valuable from that point of view. We had talked to his people before, during the whole debacle of working on **Grace Under Pressure**, that bad experience with

Steve Lillywhite, but it didn't work out from a scheduling point of view."

Geddy responds to Neil's supposition that both **Presto** and **Roll the Bones** focused somewhat on an extreme dynamic, this idea of quiet acoustic parts placed next to much louder full-band workouts. "Well, every album for me is different; it just turns out that I tried to focus on a different aspect of writing and arranging. Some of them are more about verses, and some of them are more about choruses [laughs]. Some of them are more about dynamics.

"Certainly when we started working with Peter Collins, he was very much into that Trevor Horn school of dynamics, with exaggerated changes of scenery from verse to chorus to link; **Power Windows** is a very good example of that. All kinds of sounds are utilized to mark every new part of a song. That was a really interesting experiment because I think we had a tendency to want to write that way anyway, on some of our earlier albums. But when we first entered into that whole synthesizer mode, rather than go angular, we kind of went linear and started bulking up the density of our sound; **Signals** and **Grace Under Pressure** are very dense records, in some ways. And when we started working with Peter, he brought in this whole attitude of angular production, which I liked a lot. It was a bit more concerned with audio candy, in a way, emphasizing different parts of songs by using a different kind of dynamic or scene change. He used to use the term 'scene change' a lot. So that record and **Hold Your Fire**, probably to a lesser degree, were kind of working in that mode.

"And then with Rupert on **Presto** and **Roll the Bones**, we kept that same attitude, but it was softened, because he's much more of a singer-songwriter. So the focus became more on good melodies, good chorus melodies. And I learned a lot from him in terms of singing; he was a very good singing coach and a very good singing producer. And I think he's had good success producing singers in the past; he's worked with an incredible variety of men and women. And he showed me things about

the way I enunciate that creates certain sounds, so I liked it. They were a great team to work with.

"I think the songwriting on **Presto** is inferior to **Roll the Bones**," sums up Geddy. "I think we experimented with some things on **Presto** that came to fruition on **Roll the Bones**. In a way, **Presto** is a warm-up to **Roll the Bones**. I think there's some very, very strong songs on **Roll the Bones**, and I can't say that's true for **Presto**, you know, outside of *The Pass* and a couple of others. I don't think it's our strongest album from a writing point of view."

Only five songs from the album — *Superconductor, Show Don't Tell, The Pass,* The Police-like *War Paint* and *Scars* (Talking Heads funk?) — would be played on the **Presto** tour, a five-month jaunt that would cover all of America and large Canadian markets only, the band determined not to be on the road too long. The Toronto stand would raise $200,000 for United Way; staff back at the office printed up "I Survived Rush Playing Toronto"

shirts, due to all the demands put on the band for complimentary tickets and such. Mr. Big, featuring Buffalo bass legend Billy Sheehan (also of Talas and David Lee Roth), would provide most of the support. "Good friends, good musicians, good people," says Neil, with Geddy adding that "Billy Sheehan was a terrific bass player. I was always aware of him, and he's still just a monster bass player." Voivod (Rush with fangs?) was called upon to play in Quebec. Of note, that band's acclaimed **Angel Rat** album from '91 would be produced by none other than Terry Brown.

"The most memorable thing was the big bunnies, the giant inflatable bunnies on tour," says Neil about what turned out, by all accounts, to be a most enjoyable trek. "That was very amusing, the good bunny and the bad bunny. Because the title was **Presto**, which I had used in an ironic sense, in wishing that I had magic powers to make things right in the song. And I really just liked the word. So we chose that as the title, and then again I think Hugh Syme came up with the idea of the bunnies making themselves come out of hats. So in the production design for that tour, we were playing off of that as a prop, and we got two inflatable bunnies, 40 feet tall or something. There was the good one and the bad one, and there was an animated movie of the bad bunny shooting the good bunny, who collapses. It was a whole theater . . . the theater absurdo [laughs]."

But the specific plot around good bunny versus bad bunny, Geddy explains, didn't come until later. "The bunnies were the big deal on that tour; everybody loved the bunnies. They were just a matter of coming up with the idea and having them executed and working on the timing with respect to inflating them and deflating them.

"The best bunny story I have is that, after we used them for a couple of tours, it was hard to put them away because people loved them so much [laughs]. But after we used them on two tours, it was like, 'Guys, we can't just keep trotting these bunnies out.' And somebody said, 'It's time we killed the gag.' And I said, 'Yeah, why don't we do that?' I have this group of people that are involved in the preproduction every year — Norm Stangl from Spin Productions and a few other people — and every year he helps me create a team of animators or visual people that we discuss ideas with for rear-screen films. We were sitting around talking . . . 'Is there something we can do with the bunnies?' And we decided we would go all evil on the bunnies, make one an evil bunny and make one a good bunny, and we would literally kill the gag by having one of the bunnies pop up and suddenly, instead of being a sweet cuddly thing, be this evil one with a gun. And he would raise the gun and fire a bullet, and the bullet would hit the screen and be animated, and we would go on this little animated journey with this bullet, looking for the good bunny. And it actually turned out to be a really clever bit of animation; it's one of my favorite pieces that we had designed. In the end, the good bunny rises, then the bad bunny comes up, fires the gun, a puff of smoke, and this cartoon starts, where there's this bullet that has a personality, and it goes through all kinds of wacky . . . it was really loony tunes. And then it hits good bunny, which deflates.

"Well, you could hear the crowd go 'Oohhhh.' I mean, they didn't like us killing the bunny [laughs]. So it was a really bizarre little gag that came out of the dark corners of our creative ability. And to this day, I can remember people being so disappointed that we actually shot the bunny on stage."

The bunny joke was taken a step forward. In each city, the band's production office would order up some impromptu "Playboy" bunnies (not official ones) to emerge from the side stage and give Alex and Geddy a

peck on the cheek and a wipe of the brow and serve them both some much-needed refreshments.

In terms of visuals, the band carried with them a full laser setup, most impressive for the running laser man of *Marathon*. *The Pass* utilized excellent black-and-white rear screen imagery. *Subdivisions* featured the classic video footage from seven years previous.

On the tour, when away from bunnies of all types, Alex and Geddy played tennis virtually every day off. Amusingly, Alex had his painting materials brought up to his room every day but never ended up addressing this side of his artistic self once throughout the jaunt. Neil had set up an intriguing regimen with his bicycling. His schedule included the quest for America's cheapest motel. After a show, the band would take off on the bus, then drop Neil off in the middle of the night at one of these motels an hour or so from the next city on the tour schedule. Neil would then bike in the next day. Things didn't go according to plan one time in Salt Lake City, during which Neil ended up having to bike over a mountain. At nightfall. Through snow. On a less messy note, Geddy (and sometimes Neil) would go to art galleries. Both Neil and Geddy are collectors of fine art books, but Geddy was also known for buying a considerable amount of fine art photography.

Finally, it must be said that it was in Andrew MacNaughtan's job description for the **Presto** tour (along with official photographer, personal assistant and various additional video duties as time went on) to "keep the band entertained." As entertainment director, he led the band through a

succession of costumes, silly hats and, at one point, a threesome of afro wigs, which even made it off the bus and onto soundcheck. As well, inspired by the 1988 Richard Dreyfuss movie *Moon over Parador*, the band had to be equipped with exotic, sweet, fruity "Puna" drinks, which of course led to a continuous search for the craziest, most unusual drinking glasses from which to sip them, funny hat on head required.

Roll
the Bones

As Geddy alludes to, Roll the Bones is the actualization of the somewhat aseptic searching experienced on Presto. There's an assured sense of purpose on this one. The tooling and the language are the same, yet the songs remain fixed to the memory banks longer, perhaps due to a propensity for stronger choruses, not to mention the bolder sound picture.

The title track stands as the record's ageless classic, its stunning wash of acoustic guitars supporting a clear and clean lyric from Peart that is a crowd highlight of many a Rush show. The term "roll the bones" means roll the dice, dice being made of tusk, or bone. The implications around the ideas of choice and chance are obvious, but Neil also remarked at the time that one could look at it as an exhortation to get out and do, as in getting the ol' bones rolling, making records and touring them.

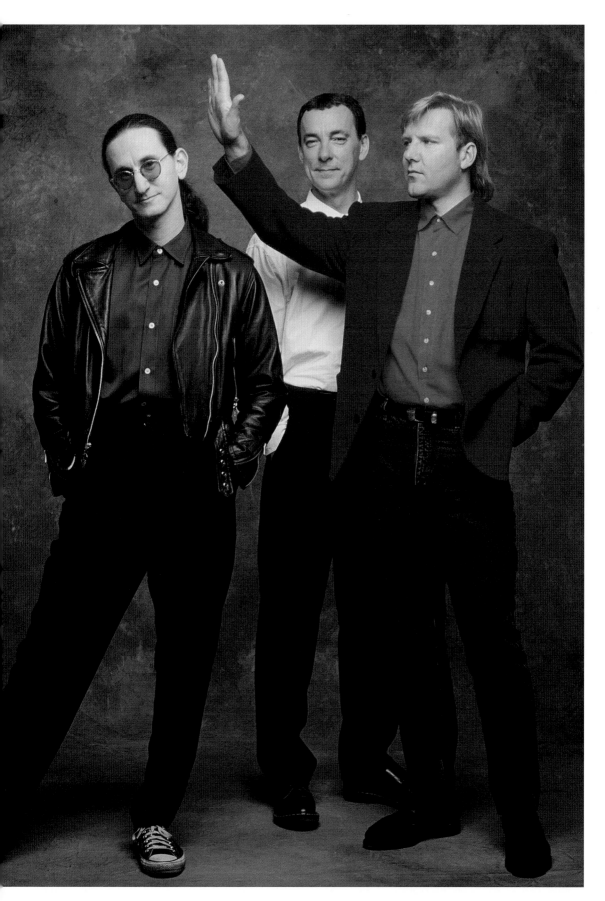

Bravado — during press done at the time, it was Geddy's favorite, due to its spontaneity — recalls the emotional sublimity of *The Pass* (even though Neil is exceedingly busy), while opener *Dreamline* is similarly morose, strafed by a crouching-then-striking verse and clouds-breaking chorus. It is a track that proved to be strong enough to open the **Different Stages** live album seven years later and then stay tenaciously in the set for the **Vapor Trails** tour.

Much of the back half of the record is springy, unadorned guitar pop, featuring some of Peart's finest lyrics. *Heresy* includes a drum rhythm Neil had heard in his African travels as well as some innovative guitar sounds from Alex. Lyrically, the song is an interesting take on the fall of the Berlin Wall, the idea that, even though it looked like a celebration, the larger message is really about what a waste this whole experiment was (of energy, effort, resources, brainpower, lives). Then there's an instrumental called *Where's My Thing?*, which rhythm-machines along deep into the memory circuits, Alex's cluster of funk chords being the track's brilliant central tenet.

"**Roll the Bones** is one of the ones that still remains really satisfying; it's just a good selection of songs," says Neil, studying the back of the CD case, glasses added to check the fine print. "They have different satisfactions. *Dreamline* I really liked because I was able to write verses that were imagistic and nonrhyming, freeing myself from my usual neatness habits. *Bravado* is a song where I just loved the music and the words married. That's one of our more successful overall compositions

— arrangement, performance, all of that wedded together. *Roll the Bones* I really liked. It's from an ongoing series of songs that is our attempt to weld together diverse styles into the same song. Sometimes it works, sometimes it doesn't, but it's obviously something that interests all of us as an ongoing pattern of song construction. And I had a lot of fun doing the rap section in the middle of that tune. This was out in '91 or so, so, yeah, rap was just starting to become increasingly prevalent then. So I just did a kind of tongue-in-cheek thing that I really like. And other songs . . . *Face Up* is one of the songs that we didn't think lived up to the potential hope we had for it. *Ghost of a Chance* is one of our all-time good ones, and *You Bet Your Life*, I particularly like the lyrics in that one. I wove together all the different religions and musical styles and everything. Those kinds of things are really fun and satisfying. Yeah, I like that one." Of note, Geddy had called *You Bet Your Life* one of the most difficult tracks to assemble on the album, specifically in the mixing stage, due to the density of the chorus.

On the promotional trail for the album, Alex was more than pleased that the band was able to put the album together so quickly, indeed finishing two months ahead of schedule, where previously a day or two early was a happy circumstance. He also indicated that some of his guitar solos for the record were the originals from the eight-track demos, specifically those for *Bravado* and *Ghost of a Chance*, which hit #1 on the US rock radio chart. The release date for the album was subsequently moved up a couple of months, and this time out there was less

talk of quitting the road. Indeed, the guys had a tight schedule worked out clear to the release of the next album. But first came what was still the usual grind, a grind that, as they say of the ocean, deserved wary respect.

For the **Roll the Bones** tour, Rush would be back to full strength, hitting the road for eight months, with Hamilton (Andy Curran from Anthem act Coney Hatch as backup), down the road an hour from Toronto and actually Neil's birthplace, serving as tour opener on October 25th, 1991. **Roll the Bones** received its gold certification in the US the same day as well, on the heels of opening at #3 on Billboard, the highest album placement of the band's career. Otherwise, the tour included a handful of other central Canadian dates, only Vancouver in the west, and then the band's usual blanket coverage of America. A typical stint of about a month in Europe included an even split between Germany and the UK, with Rotterdam and Paris filling out the trek. The band insisted, for their Berlin stand, that they stay in a hotel in East Berlin (rather than West Berlin) given that the wall had come down two years previous.

Halfway around the world, the band ended up having one of their worst shows ever, at least from an onstage anger standpoint. Rush refused to play general admission shows due to the potential for injury and even death in the crowd. In Sacramento, somehow, the show ended up being general admission, and the crowd was unruly to say the least. Throughout the set by backup band Primus, everything from shoes to water bottles to beach balls and other bottles was flying, and the melee continued for Rush. At one point, Geddy got hit in the face with a shoe, which then landed on his pedals and set off a sample to a different song than the one they were playing. The band fumed throughout the rest of the set, and much shouting and slamming of locker doors could be heard backstage afterward as well.

The Tragically Hip chimed in as backup for a hometown show on December 16th, 1991, once again as a United Way benefit, with the Daily Bread Food Bank also ending up with 15,000 pounds of crowd-donated food. Axe-shredder Vinnie Moore supported, as did Mr. Big. Guitarist Eric Johnson handled the first leg of the tour, and avant-garde anti-power-trio Primus jumped on for the first of their two terms with the band.

"Eric was another one where I would go out and watch him almost every night as well," recalls Alex fondly. "His playing is so articulate but still very soulful. He and I are a year and a day apart in our birthdays, so we had a Virgo thing [laughs]. We jammed a couple of times in the tuning room and spent a few evenings just talking about other nonmusical things. He's quite a spiritual guy. I gave him my double-neck guitar as a gift, and about a month after I gave it to him one of the crew guys who had quite a drug problem and was quite ill stole it and sold it, and that was heartbreaking. I mean, that was a special gift."

With respect to the tour's set list, *Distant Early Warning* was dropped in time for the European leg, replaced by *Red Sector A*. *Subdivisions* was replaced by *Vital Signs* at the same time, *The Pass* replaced by *The Analog Kid* as well. Late in the tour, the band added a *Cygnus X-1* teaser at the close of the show, with *The Trees* added for the American dates after the European tour, the third leg as it were, if the second leg could be called the appendage starting January 18th, '92, after nearly a month's break. For the encore, there was a medley that took in *The Spirit of Radio*, *Overture* from *2112*, *Finding My Way*, *La Villa Strangiato*, *Anthem*, *Red Barchetta* and then finally back to *Spirit* again. From **Roll the Bones**, *Ghost of a Chance* was a late arrival, joining clear choices *Dreamline*, *Bravado*, *Where's My Thing?* and *Roll the Bones*.

Surround sound technology was used — at the sole control or responsibility of one Robert Scovill — namely speakers in all four corners of each venue lit upon. This was most impressively heard with respect to the

electronic drum lick that both opens and closes *Force Ten*, as well as within Neil's drum solo, Scovill creating a 360-degree run of the bases, as it were.

"The film was a big one with . . . the skull singing the rap section," says Neil when asked about other distinguishing features on the **Roll the Bones** tour, Rush lifting the footage from the amusing and successful video. "I don't think there was anything else, particularly, production-wise that I remember. We still had the bunnies on that tour, I think; we hadn't retired them yet [laughs]."

Geddy, ever the film guy, points out an additional dimension. "That's when we got into the whole computer thing; that was the whole CGI revolution, with the computer graphics. And the great thing with being involved in the visual production is that you learn so much about different animation techniques. And we experimented with some different kinds of animators over the years. Even going back to the early, early stuff, through the **Power Windows** and **Hold Your Fire** period, we used all kinds of different young animators in Toronto to do things. For *Manhattan Project*, there was a really great animated piece done. Even *Red Lenses* we had this wacky, wacky cartoon done for it. And so that's something that really intrigued me.

"So when it came time to do something for *Roll the Bones*, I can't remember where the idea came from, but the whole talking skull idea popped up. It was a major production coming up with the people that could animate the skull in the right way, do computer graphics plus real-time animation. So we used three to four different styles of animation in the film. But also it forced us to perform songs in a different way. In

order for the animation to come on at the right time and for the skeleton to do the rap, we had to play to a click, just so the timing all worked, which was kind of nightmarish for Neil. But that began that whole thing where we would do that. We had done that a little bit in the past, when we played *Time Stand Still*, and that's how Amy's voice used to appear nightly, as magic, while she appeared on the film."

One thing the guys recall fondly is their time spent with Primus, Les Claypool and company providing mind expansion on both the **Roll the Bones** and **Counterparts** tours. "Les is amazing, a great stylist," notes Geddy. "I like the way he plays, and I like his inventiveness. He's not a traditional riff guy, and I usually adore the riff guys. But he brings a whole different, incredibly inventive style to playing bass."

Alex gives his account of the legendary Primus-Rush sessions — coming to a box set near you? "The deal was you had to go out and get an instrument or instruments that you don't know how to play. That's what we would do. So after our soundcheck, we'd come back and have dinner. They would do their soundcheck, they'd come back. And from that

kind of six to seven slot, we would jam. We bought a flute, harmonica, a clarinet, some weird drums, all just cheap stuff from pawnshops. And we would jam for this hour. We did it every day; it was just a riot. It was the most bizarre music you could imagine. And we started recording some of it. I don't know where those tapes ended up. But I know there are these tapes kicking around with probably 20 hours of these crazy jams, from Berlin, from America. They're probably sitting somewhere at the bottom of a case. You don't think about it at the time. . . ."

"We had a little practice drum kit for that," adds Neil. "Alex would go to pawn shops and come in with a flute or a violin. And there'd be bicycles, pipes; everybody was playing something. And pretty well every day we just had that kind of free-form blowout." Geddy was said to have played acoustic guitar and drum, Neil bongos, and Alex accordion, triangle, plus a mean set of plumbing fixtures, given that some of these esteemed (steamed?) sessions actually occurred in shower stalls.

With respect to extracurricular activities at this point in the band's career, widening interests were indeed being indulged. No matter how far away the band was from the center of the universe on any given Sunday, Geddy and Neil both insisted on the Sunday *New York Times* to be on their rooms' doorsteps that morning since both were avid attackers of its challenging crossword. Alex had become serious about golf on the **Presto** tour, and by the time **Roll the Bones** rolled around Geddy was often playing as well, Alex credited with having converting him to the joys of the game. Neil, on the other hand, had taken up archery; he and various crewmembers would find a long hallway at the venue, or a suitable area outdoors, and set up for target practice. Indeed, they had indulged in the sport at a giant castle the band stayed at in Birmingham. As well, in advance of the band's April 15th date in Glasgow, Alex and Robert Scovill set out for the local, world-famous, ocean-fronting golf course for a round in blustery, near-freezing weather.

Counterparts

Reversing the jets on the band's modest, almost miniature pop explorations, Rush set about renewing ties with Peter Collins and a heavier, guitar-laden sound. Indeed, Peter had done a few heavier things in the interim, having worked with Alice Cooper, Gary Moore, Queensryche and even Suicidal Tendencies. Counterparts subsequently screams out of the gates with a groove-mad percussive flurry not seen for years, *Animate*'s warm bass and arcane, mesmerizing melody then taking the listener on a straight-line journey into one of Rush's classic tracks. "I love *Animate*," offers Geddy unequivocally. "I think it's one of the great songs we've done. There's something about the bestiality of that song, the insistence of it."

But the album's lead single would be an even heavier track (and one of those fairly regular afterthoughts), *Stick It Out* crashing into view with a huge heavy metal riff played simultaneously by Alex and Geddy, no Neil in sight until a hi-hat pattern meekly presents itself. Geddy's not so fast with the praise on this one. "You know, in retrospect, I love the riff; it's a great riff song. I love playing it, and it's a very bass-heavy song, which always makes me happy [laughs]. Lyrically, it's kind of a so-so song for us. I don't know, I think the best thing about that song is the vibe and the fact that it's stripped back down to a trio, back to doing riff rock. I think that was the important thing about that song. *Animate* is more what we were after, this combination of bringing different rhythmic attitudes back into it while trying to add a bit more funk at the same time but be big-bottomed and aggressive."

Nobody's Hero, quite contrastingly, opens with plaintive acoustic guitar, warm chording then arriving, while Geddy sings a dedication to the real heroes of the world, most of them unsung (until now), often because their heroism was infinitely intense to the point of being immeasurable or perhaps unfathomable o'er a TV screen. *Between Sun & Moon* is a heavy rocker with additional welcome Peart percussive lubrications, propelling a third collaboration between Neil and Pye Dubois. Come solo time, Alex twangs and clangs forthrightly. *Double Agent* similarly contains joyous, muscular drumming among mischievous chords from Lifeson; it is a track where caution is thrown to the wind, indeed, the song thrown

together near the end of the **Counterparts** process. If it's even possible, sequel *Leave That Thing Alone* is an even funkier instrumental than "quel" *Where's My Thing?* given the unfair advantage of the wider record's full spectrum recording, namely some bass. Finally, *Cold Fire* is quite simply an under-heralded Rush classic, with its gorgeous verse melody exploding into one of the most insistent Rush choruses in years.

"**Counterparts** was definitely a reaction against that whole keyboard thing; there's no question in my mind," says Geddy. "We had pushed that to the limit. I would say through the end of working with Rupert, and having now done two or three tours in this kind of slavish live mode, I think I was starting to have some frustration, and I know Alex was really starting to have some frustration. And I think the writing of **Counterparts** reflected that. That's why there's very little keyboards on that record, kind of token keyboards. And, really, they're not even necessary when I hear them, the little bits of keyboard parts that are still there. It's kind of a habit that was dying hard.

"**Counterparts** brought Pete back, which was fun. It was great to work with him again, after having not done two records with him. And our decision not to work with Peter had nothing to do with Peter. It was strictly a desire to keep learning and to keep moving. Working with Pete introduced us to the concept of learning from other people. If we were still going to be a band after all these years, maybe we have to change the people around us from time to time so that we keep learning new stuff.

So that's all that was, and working with Rupert and Stephen really did accomplish that. But I think there was something about Pete that we missed.

"We brought in this guy, Kevin Shirley, 'The Caveman,' to engineer too, who at the time was kind of a little-known guy that Peter had stumbled upon by recommendation. Of course now he's gone on to do very well for himself. And he had a very different attitude than previous engineers we worked with. He was a real analog, opinionated, big hand, big sound guy. And I think he was great for that project. I think it's one of our best-sounding records. I think he did a terrific job recording it. And we did it all in Toronto. That's where we finally said we're tired of moving around the world. Let's go back to doing it locally, at home.

"I like **Counterparts**, but it's an odd record for me. Lyrically, it has a very odd mood, but I think what I like about that record more than anything is the sound of it. It has a nice bold, ballsy sound. But I find the material a little spotty."

Alex usually wrinkles his nose at the mention of **Counterparts** as well. "There was something about it that just wasn't quite 100%. I don't know if it was the songwriting or how we approached the recording. It was a very stripped-down sort of record for us to make, and I don't know if we were completely committed to that idea. There's some great stuff on there, and there's other stuff that could have been better. Well, I can say that about any one of these records. And the mixing was OK. Again we had some conflict in ideas about how we heard it individually. I would say in the scheme of difficulty and ease it's probably somewhere in the middle, whereas **Hemispheres** and especially **Grace Under Pressure** would be in the more difficult area."

On other occasions, Alex has hinted in stronger terms about the band's disconnection at the time, intimating that it would be higher up that difficulty scale than stated in the above quotation. Geddy has admitted to having had numerous major arguments with Alex. Neil seems to strike that tone as well, agreeing that an always shifting, gray-scale

majority of the band was none too pleased with the experience. "I didn't like the making of it that much, but I like a lot of the results" is his summation. "Again not everything lives up to its potential, but *Animate* I still like; *Nobody's Hero* was good. *Alien Shore*, I like the lyrics to that particularly; *Speed of Love* likewise."

Does Neil view it as one of the heavier Rush albums, at least post-**Moving Pictures**? "Yeah, and with a lot of dark experiments, which is good. *Leave That Thing Alone* is our best-ever instrumental, so I don't think you can knock that. And *Cold Fire*, to me, is one of my most satisfying songs, musically and lyrically, although it's stuck at the second-to-last track there. Obviously, nobody else shared my high opinion of it [laughs], but it's one I really love. And again you love a song for small things. I had been inspired, I think, by a Paul Simon song, where I wanted to couch song lyrics in conversation — he said, she said, and all that. He has a song, maybe on **Rhythm of the Saints**, where it's in conversation. She said blah blah blah, and I said blah blah blah. And I thought, yeah, what a cool idea; I'd like to try something like that. And *Cold Fire* achieved that. I thought about it for a couple of years, and with this song I finally got it. I like the nature of it; it's a very grown-up relationship song. And relationship songs are never easy to do, convincingly anyway, as opposed to love songs. Relationship songs are by definition much more clinical, but this was one, I thought, that managed to be a grown-up one, with the mystified guy and the smart girl. I like the subtext of that — the guy is kind of dumb, and she's really smart and cynical [laughs]." In press at the time, Neil alluded to the term "counterparts" as housing many meanings, one of which was how the personalities of the band's three distinct individuals bounce off each other, ultimately

finding holistic balance or synergy. And, of course, there's the male/female duality addressed on more songs on this album than most others from the catalog.

The **Counterparts** tour, marking 20 years as a band for these 40ish guys, would be quick and tidy by Rush standards, comprising essentially four months of work throughout America, from late January of '94 to early May, closing off with two Quebec dates and a hometown stand. Indeed, it would be a well-received affair, the album shipping gold simultaneously in the US and Canada. Backup would come from The Doughboys (Montreal), I Mother Earth (Toronto) and Melvins (California), with Primus logging the most dates, Candlebox the second most, of which Neil recalled that "we had them for a while — nice guys. I liked one of their songs a lot too. I don't know what happened to them."

The **Counterparts** shows would open to the strains of Strauss's *Thus Spoke Zarathustra*, which then gave way to the clarion *Dreamline*. From the new album, *Stick It Out* and *Double Agent* were intensified with bursts of pyro. Other tracks that made the grade were *Animate*, *Cold Fire*, *Nobody's Hero* and *Leave That Thing Alone*, leaving fully *Cut to the Chase*, *Between Sun & Moon*, *Alien Shore*, *The Speed of Love* and *Everyday Glory* off the set list. Stage design included, in synergy with the **Counterparts** cover art, a digital and very phallic merging (and then co-screwing) of a nut and bolt, all set to dramatic prerecorded music, as well as large-sized nuts and bolts positioned around the stage.

Test for Echo

Back a reasonable three years after the last album (yet with a year-and-a-half vacation included), Rush uncoiled *Test for Echo*, a record that pleasantly balances the songwriting focal points of the Rupert Hine albums with the guitars of *Counterparts*. As well, in two bold moves, drums were recorded in upstate New York at Bearsville, and hard alternative icon Andy Wallace was brought in for mixing duties (and everywhere the band was sure to go, it snowed like crazy). Wallace, who has worked with dozens of bands, from Faith No More, Rage Against the Machine, The Cult and Slayer to Korn, Disturbed, Mudvayne and System of a Down, was ushered in as an objective ear after the band worried that they had layered things too densely again, a concern previously harbored most forthrightly during the *Signals* and *Grace* period.

Whoever was the cause of it, there's an intimate, high-fidelity sound that softens songs that could arguably be stacked against those of **Counterparts** decibel for decibel. With the industry buzzing about alternative rock at the time, some couldn't help viewing Rush in elliptical relation to that term. After all, **Test for Echo** had guitars. And Geddy, always one to keep an ear to the new music, cited in the press an admiration for Soundgarden and Smashing Pumpkins. Indeed, tracks like *Time and Motion* are wall-to-wall malevolent guitars, and *Driven* goes to those sinister, axe-mad places as well, even if its chorus is powerful yet joyous. Also on the joyous tack, *Half the World* is a hemisphere of dreamy electricity, while *The Color of Right* is similarly melodic and politely loud. Off to the back half, and there's the same exotic mix of stops and starts, acoustics against electrics, mean, snorting chording and airtight pop. *Virtuality* is bound to sound dated, given its Internet theme, and *Dog Years* is not Neil at his best, no surprise, given that he was somewhat hungover when penning it. Both sure do rock, though. On the other hand, *Resist* is a rare lush ballad for Rush, and surging instrumental *Limbo* is near-modern-era King Crimsonian at times, other times of an older, more magisterial bent.

But the end effect is of a solidly cohesive album, one with the production as a common thread, notably Alex's tidy, almost modest yet pervasive multitracked power chordings placed upon precise tones from both Geddy and Neil. It is indeed a soft rain of sounds, utilized on songs that are almost all heavy rock by loving nurture.

"**Test for Echo** was an extension of what we had been doing for so many

years," explains Alex, who considered the placement of guitars in the mix just right, definitely there but not invasive. "It was a very enjoyable record to make. There was a nice, even, calm energy to the record, very much like **Moving Pictures** was. In fact, we often compare the two in terms of how they were made and how they felt. To my ear now, **Test** is a little lighter, a little more shiny, a little more rhythmic . . . very rhythmic."

To reiterate, Alex is somewhat of a constant on the album, yet it's a new sound yet again versus the earthy thump of **Counterparts**. In fact, **Test for Echo** would be Alex's second album of 1996, having released in January of that year **Victor**, his first solo album, aided by Les Claypool and a host of local names, including his son Adrian. Let's not forget that Neil has been toiling away on drum-historical solo albums, instructional videos, travel books and, necessary to the latter, an incredible amount of quite brave travel.

"Alex is a guy who gets bored very quickly," notes Geddy, when asked to nail a single characteristic of his axe-slinging cohort, whose aforementioned **Victor** album could be viewed as Rush with an acidic tongue, a cacophonous sense of mission, Rush music made by a bunch of guys who are adequate facsimiles save for vocals. "He's never been a purist about playing guitar. He doesn't really like a simple guitar sound, and he doesn't like to play parts that are in any way conventional. So he spends a lot of his time thinking about different ways of grappling with distortion. And he utilizes a lot of effects to try to give himself a unique character. Sometimes that's very difficult to record. But most of Alex's sound comes from his fingers. It comes from the different kinds of chords and patterns that he invents, which to me are very unique. I think Alex is a great soloist, but what I think he really excels at as a guitarist is as someone who invents really great arpeggios. That aspect of his guitar playing, I think, is very underrated. I think when people realize that they are listening to one part of a song that sounds like three guitars, and it's really one part, I think it's really easy to take that for granted, because you just think it's an overdubbed thing. He invents some amazing patterns — in particular arpeggio patterns — which again, I think, is one of his greatest strengths as a guitarist."

Geddy goes on to explain the meaning of the term "test for echo," the title track being yet another collaboration with Pye Dubois. "You might get a different answer from Neil, but for me it's a call and response. You know, 'Is anybody out there?' And not only in the sense of outer space. It's like that phrase Will Farrell used in that movie, 'Am I taking crazy pills?!' You know, am I the only one that sees the insanity in this? It's a little bit about that, and it's a little bit about 'Is anybody listening?' For me, that's what the song says. It's like a view of things that are happening in our culture through the eyes of the instant media that we get and the things that we see that are not right. And yet it's still going on, still exploited. So it's about a lot of things, but to me it's an out-of-control media culture thing." Musically, the track is a wonderful jumble of disparate parts, pop next to dervish-like windup, next to laid-back, near-cavernous and quite soulful verse, then back around again.

"You could probably figure that out better than me," laughs Geddy when asked to stop and take stock of the different phases the Rush sound has gone through up to this point. "I guess I see ourselves as one band, really. But we've gone through an evolution. I see Rush as a continuing experiment, to be honest. But it's not like it's so inaccessible, like fusion jazz or something. There's still a basic rock/metal thing, so we're still accessible. But I'd say the first period, up to **2112**, we were a band

desperate to find our own voice. And I think **2112** marked the creation of our own sound for the first time really. And I think the next period, up until and beyond **Moving Pictures**, we were still exploring our new sound, but I think our confidence grew, and the complexities became more overt in what we were doing. And then we went through a very textural period, a synthesizer-influenced period with **Power Windows** and **Hold Your Fire**, which began with **Signals**. That was where the band went from a three-piece, hard rock, progressive band into acting more like a four-piece band; that was a fairly profound change in attitude for us. And I would say that the last two or three albums have been an effort to kind of take what we learned through that four-piece period and try to reestablish a three-piece architecture. It's kind of like a weaning off of the elements that we learned. By going through that keyboard period, we learned a lot about songwriting. So I think we are trying to apply those things we learned but within a more direct structure."

Geddy summed up the creative process within Rush as it existed in the late '90s. "With Rush, we have a good time, we laugh, but there's this quiet — what's the best word to describe this? — this quiet structure around us. And that structure is the band and the workings of the band. And although we're really good at not paying a whole lot of attention to it, it's still there. Even when you are writing for writing's sake, or music for music's sake, it's still me, Alex and Neil and the personalities of our

instruments that are imposed on the work. And when you are outside of that, working with other people perhaps, and it's just a couple of guys sitting around trying to write some music that they find compelling, you're out of the box, you know? And as subtle as the box may be, you're out of it."

"No, let's start with the album," laughs Neil when pressed for his memories of the **Test for Echo** tour. "I really like that one. Again, as a fan, this would probably be my favorite of the '90s albums. Yet there are some special circumstances with this.

"I started working with my drum teacher, Freddie Gruber, just before this. We had some time off while Geddy and Nancy were having a baby, and I did the Buddy Rich tribute, and was working with all these different great drummers, and met Freddie through Steve Smith. So I started studying with Freddie, to where I started practicing every day with all these different exercises that he had given me for the physical motion on the drums and so on. So I spent more than a year, 18 months I think, practicing drums every day. So by the time we came to **Test for Echo**, I was playing a completely different style. That's one of the things that I did willingly with Freddie. I thought, OK, after 25 years at that time, 30 years maybe, let's try something new.

"So I surrendered and went back to traditional grip, turned the sticks around and played them properly and learned all his techniques of physical motion. So I came into this not only at a really high technical peak but as a reinvented musical creature too. And the telling point was, when I first started playing along with the demos and all that, Geddy and Alex were saying, 'It doesn't sound that much different to me.' And the producer, Peter Collins, said, 'It still sounds like you.' But when I recorded the drum parts, and they were playing to them, they noticed the clock was different. They had to adjust their playing. Again that subtle thing I talked about before, about nailing feels and tempos and so on; I had subtly changed my clock, my driving metronome, in the gyroscope of all my drum playing. That forced them to change theirs. So that's an example of how far-reaching the subtleties — all the subtleties — were. So that was a really important record for me.

"I made the instructional video after that, *A Work in Progress*," continues Neil, "and talked about the concept of creating a masterpiece in the true sense, the way it used to be, in the days of the apprentices. If you wanted to be accepted as a master in the guild, you had to create a piece of work; whether you're a stonemason or a guilder or carver or whatever, that was your masterpiece. You'd put it before the masters to be accepted among them and to end your apprenticeship, as it were. So I was talking about

it in those terms, really, trying, always, to achieve something that was worthy of your ideal judge, if you were setting up a master in your guild to approve or not of your work. Then your work was necessarily, within the craft, an attempt to achieve that mastery."

The **Test for Echo** tour saw the band spend October '96 until the end of the year covering a large chunk of America, with the Yuletide season spent in Ontario and Quebec (December 18th saw the band play a Molson-sponsored club gig in Toronto as part of the beer brand's Blind Date promotion). May '97 saw a similar jaunt start up, again through all parts of the US and again winding up in central Canada to close things out in late June and early July. The **Test for Echo** dates were billed as "An Evening with Rush," meaning no backup act, Rush playing for a super-human two and a half to three hours every night, traveling by private jet for the first time ever, a well-deserved perk given the nightly workout.

"That was the first tour we did that way," says Geddy, "where there was no opening act and we had two sets. So we could actually indulge ourselves a little bit and try to invent some sort of dramatic or at least teasing beginning to the second set. And we used *Test for Echo* to open that second set, I believe. The big kind of production for that tour was the film that we made for that song. We had fun using some kind of multi-media thing, exploiting the concept of that song into a fine combo of video and sound."

On the subject of Rush's backup acts, a situation from this point on that is no more, it's been obvious that the band has gotten a great deal of

pleasure and indeed gathered — if mostly by osmosis — substantive musical knowledge from the bands with which they've "shared the experience." For Geddy, however, that has been quite exclusively a bass-playing interchange, at least when it came to the heavier metal bands. "I didn't like most of those bands, to be frank. The heavy rock bands that played with us, the lead singers, were always so operatic and so overblown to me; it never really appealed to me. I like the way Kim sings, from Max. I think he's a good vocalist, underrated; he's got a lot of expression and a nice tone."

Back on the **Test for Echo** tour, the band also utilized an increasingly sophisticated array of live camera footage, complex video, lasers and strobes. The shows opened once again with the *Thus Spoke Zarathustra* intro music, followed by *Dreamline*. Tracks from the new album that made the first of the band's two sets were *Driven*, *Half the World*, *Limbo* and *Virtuality*. An intermission followed, featuring B-movie trailers and the ubiquitous drive-in classic *Let's All Go to the Lobby and Have Ourselves a Snack*. The **Test for Echo** tracks in the second set were the title track, *Time and Motion* and *Resist*, although the latter two only on occasion. *The Big Money* would be replaced by *Limelight* for the second half of the tour, likewise the impromptu *Wipeout!* replaced with *Stick It Out*. *Subdivisions* would be dropped for the second leg, with *Red Sector A* getting moved from the first to the second set.

As Neil is wont to say, as the years went on, his life "got bigger." It was the same with everybody in the band. On tour up into the **Counterparts** and **Test for Echo** years, any number of activities would fill out the days of the guys. Upon being asked if Geddy had become a pretty serious book collector, Alex replies that "I think to a degree he is; I don't know. He's a collector, period. He collects wine, he collects baseball memorabilia, books. He's the kind of guy who gets very interested in something and likes to really learn as much as he can about it, and Neil is the same way.

"If Neil's into something, he will exhaust it before he moves on to something else. When he got into motorcycles, for example, he really got into motorcycles. Now he does a motorcycle tour when we're touring. He rides 30,000 miles on a tour, and he writes his journals, based on his experience on the bike. He did the same thing with cycling — he got so into cycling.

"Writing for him, writing these travel journals, has become a really big thing. You know, he published for the first time on the last tour, but he's been writing these things for years now. He does a short, limited run of maybe 150 books for his friends. So he's been learning how to do that and building up the confidence to have finally released a major work. With his last book, **Ghost Rider**, I mean, the material he had to work with was so powerful. But I think he really learned how to put it into print by doing all those other things. He's always been super, super focused, quite disciplined.

"The last two tours he had the motorcycle," clarifies Alex, on Peart's extensive itinerary, "**Test for Echo** and **Vapor Trails**. Prior to that, I think he cycled at least two tours, if not three. And he did other bike trips. He did one throughout Europe, Africa, China; he really got into the bike thing. And for him, it's the perfect thing. He's not into sports. He doesn't

play any sports at all. He's very uncoordinated, which is great for a drummer [laughs] but not for a tennis player. But he's quite clumsy otherwise. But cycling for him, because he's a solitary kind of guy. . . . Maybe less so now, but in the past he really enjoyed his private time. He would get on his bike and ride out 50 or 60 miles and ride back — nobody but him. He could focus on his — whatever you would call it — cadence, the tempo of his bike riding. A little bit the same as motorcycling. He could shut out the rest of the world and focus on staying on the road, you know, looking out for other cars. This is his kind of escape and how he dealt with being on the road.

"And you try to find ways to deal with being on the road in positive and constructive ways. Because it's so easy to slip into bad habits. And we're lucky. We've managed to stay away from those sort of pitfalls. But to say that we didn't come close on occasions would be inaccurate."

"I have lots of interests," adds Geddy on this subject of leading big lives. "I play tennis, I travel a lot with my family and on my own. We go to France once a year to Burgundy to do wine-tastings and things, so I'm a busy guy. I got pretty big into cycling this last summer, so I did a lot of cycling and long-distance riding. I make sure I plan at least one or two bike trips every year somewhere in the world. I'm a huge wine collector; it's a great passion to me. Literature, of course. Films — I love cinema, always have. It's always been a big interest of mine."

"**Test for Echo** was a hard but satisfying tour," notes Neil, bringing us back to the working world. "I thought we really played well on the tour, and I remember I documented this tour in journals and planned to write a book about it, so I have a lot of documentation on it. And I remember writing notes in my journal about listening to the shows and how good they were and how well Geddy was singing and how well we were playing. So that was very satisfying in that respect but at the same time grueling, physically. There were a lot of shows, and I had the elbow problem going on toward the end, so I was in pain. But we did play really well."

Neil elaborates on his injury. "The whole end of the **Test for Echo** tour I was wearing an elbow brace because I was getting tendonitis and all that. But I was so glad that I could play all right. You know, it hurt, but it would be much worse if I couldn't play right; that would be crushing. And I've never fortunately faced anything that was physically debilitating, feeling like I can't do the job. That would be an awful thing to face, much worse than a limitation of hardware or an injury. But even that injury, like I said, it hurt like hell, but I could still play right. And that's all that mattered. I made that journal note at the time."

And did it eventually heal to his satisfaction? "Oh, yeah! I had to really abuse the thing for months, night after night. You know, how many times in the course of a show do I hit something as hard as I can with my right hand? You know, thousands, tens of thousands, of times. So, yeah, there was residual pain and recovery and all that. But again I was just glad to be able to do the job, to my satisfaction at least, no matter how stupid I looked with a big elbow brace. . . . That's not the point; I'm not there to feel good [laughs]. Again, I'm not there to have fun, you know?"

I asked Neil to comment on the evolution of his drum solo up to this point. "Every tour it gets restructured and largely, I think, recomposed, at least as a framework. . . . I remember, at the beginning of **Vapor Trails**, I went back and listened to the solo I was doing on **Test for Echo**. And I thought, 'Well, I'm really not finished with that framework.' As far as I'm concerned, that's OK; I can go forward with that, and it still represents a vehicle of expression and exploration for me. And then I thought, 'No, no, I can't do that.' So I did take it all apart, and the parts that I kept I reconfigured or reorchestrated or whatever.

"But to me, it is a performance piece in that each tour has a different structure, but there's always a structure for the tour that gets built on. And I feel it's developed, as I develop certain ideas and experiment with others, in the course of it. Because it, unlike a song, has a fixed structure of turning points and transitions and movements, but the content is not structured. It's not at all remembered. I know when I switch to a mode — 'OK, this is the snare drum/bass drum part; OK, go into that.' But that's whatever comes out.

"That's a way of being structured and loose at the same time, and I've done that in the studio the last couple of records. For example, on *Resist* on **Test for Echo**, I worked and rehearsed and rehearsed and rehearsed

that song, and I worked out every possible kind of fill that might work. But I didn't allow myself to orchestrate them, so that, when I played them in the studio, I didn't know, you know? I knew what would work, but I didn't know how it was going to come out.

"So that's an example of how the drum solo is. I've worked out the structure of it and the arrangements and the transitions — that remains constant — but the content of the movements is strictly whatever comes out of me that night."

"You'd be very surprised," says Alex when questioned about the band's routine leading up to show time. "Backstage before a Rush show — and when I say backstage I mean the dressing room — is much like a library [laughs]. It's very quiet. Neil is usually sitting in a corner reading. There is no psych-up. We get dressed, we chat a little bit about whatever, and somebody comes and gets us and we go on. There's no group hug or prayer or anything like that. We just do our thing."

"I don't know; I'm not very hard to please," adds Neil when asked about food requirements, riders and such. "I like some salty peanuts and some ginger ale and a tuna sandwich on the bus [laughs]. But there's one thing; we always like to go to the show in the afternoon, for example, and do soundcheck and stay there. We always felt a certain uneasiness about leaving. There's some kind of, almost superstition, where we think that we won't get back in time for the show. So that's a pattern we established early on and we always stuck to. I don't think any of us has ever left the venue after we go there in the afternoon, whereas most people do, I think. So we were always more comfortable going to work and staying there, basically.

"So, yeah, just being able to have dinner and have a rehearsal room — those are the kinds of things for me. Just being able to have dinner when we want it, between soundcheck and the show, and having a room to warm up in. And then I leave right off the stage, so the rest of it doesn't affect me. There's a certain pattern to the day though, and you feel it winding up inside you through the course of the day. It's a show day, which is unlike any other thing. You go to the venue and do soundcheck, and then not being able to warm up . . . like when we did the big Toronto show last summer, I didn't have a warm-up kit backstage, and it upset my whole rhythm of things, so to speak. That's the kind of thing that becomes a really important part of the day, just to go in for half an hour and warm up on my little practice kit. That's not superstitious obviously, but it's important."

A career highlight for the band would take place on February 26th of '97, when Alex, Geddy and Neil were presented with their country's highest honor, the Order of Canada, both for (quietly) raising over a million dollars for charities over the years and for (loudly) being Rush.

"I don't think that after **Test for Echo** the intention was to take a very long break," says Alex, inevitably alluding to the tragedies that were to present themselves upon Neil and necessarily the band. "We enjoyed making **Test**; it was a very fun record to make, good vibe in the studio. The tour was great; doing 'An Evening with' was really a lot of fun for us. It gave us a chance to play stuff like 2112 in its entirety [*Natural Science* was brought back as well]. The tour went really, really well. We were healthy through the whole thing, and we got to the end of it fine. I think we were really planning on taking a relatively short break and then back in for the next record. No one could know that what happened would happen."

What happened is that in August of 1997 Neil's only child, daughter Selena Taylor, was killed in a car accident, at age 19. Unthinkably, Neil's inconsolable wife, Jackie, succumbed to cancer less than a year later. Subsequently, Neil expressed the unfathomably sad sentiment that Jackie, in fact, had really died of a broken heart.

"How time has affected a band like us I can't really say because it's not just time," says Alex, obviously sharing Neil's grief intensely, as much as is possible for a near and dear outsider. "It's not just the longevity, it's the impact of what happens in that time. Really, all of us questioned whether or not we'd make another record, if we would ever work again. When this all happened, the band was the very last thing on our minds. I mean, it just didn't seem appropriate to even think about it. Music's about celebration, and there was no feeling of celebration at that time. It was circle the wagons and help as much as you can. That was the foremost thing. I didn't play the guitar for over a year, I think. And I play all

the time. Neil didn't play his drums, obviously, for four years. A lot of things changed; it took a while to get out of that.

"It's just your spirit, something, just leaves," continues Alex. "And you're so overwhelmed by the depth of the grief and the pain that you see, particularly in your friends, the pain that you feel, and it changes you for sure; it changes you forever. You look at things a lot differently. I care in many different ways than I did then. I've always been a caring person, and by nature I like to help people, and I like to make people happy around me, but that took it to another level. It gave me a sense of purpose. I've had a lot of sick friends lately, and I don't know why it is, but I deal with it so much better now. Maturing is part of it, yes, but based on what your experiences are . . . boy, something like that, you really learn a lot from it.

"I think the office made some kind of group press release at the time, but we didn't get involved in any of the sites or talk to anybody directly," explains Alex when asked about the thought that maybe this would be the

end of the line for Rush. "What happened happened, and that was a personal thing. We love the support from our fans, and it was beautiful to see their reaction to what had happened and their support. But if new music was never going to happen, if that was the end of it, so be it, that's the way life goes. You can't do anything about that. We do this for ourselves. We don't do this for our fans per se, or we don't do it for the money, or we don't do it for those things. Before anything else, we do it for ourselves. I think that's the great thing about our relationship with our fans; they expect us to do that. They expect us to make mistakes, and they expect us to go to new territory. That's what they like about the relationship, and it would be disappointing to them if it ever changed."

Different Stages

R U S H
different stages · live

In late '98, despite blinding personal pain, and despite voiced thoughts that the band couldn't be pressed to produce, the Rush ball was kept rolling with a mammoth three-CD live set. The album includes a disc comprising a Hammersmith Odeon show, recorded for (but aborted as) a radio broadcast, at the back end of the A Farewell to Kings tour. The other two discs include three tracks from the Counterparts tour, a handful of other isolated and fortunate incidents, but mainly selections from the band's Chicago Test for Echo stand on June 23rd of '97, a result that Geddy at the time found quite amusing given that over a hundred shows were recorded for aural perusal. Test for Echo is represented by only three tracks, the complexion of the album looking like a hits pack with welcome smatterings from the '90s albums and '89's Presto included.

"We had been recording material for two tours," explains Geddy. "We are gathering quite an overwhelming library of material actually, and, coupled with the discovery of the tapes from 1978, it was just obvious that we needed to put a package together. And in my mind, seeing that we were coming up on 25 years as a band, I thought it was an opportune moment to put together a retrospective, in essence, from a live point of view. And because a lot of the responsibility for this project kind of gravitated into my corner, I just kind of decided what the concept was going to be."

Are there more tapes of vintage shows? "Not really, no. Nothing that I would consider to be vaguely reminiscent of that quality. The quality that we found on that particular show is remarkable for a 20-year-old analog tape recording. So I would say there's nothing really approaching that usable. But this one was an effort to go into the realm of the idealistic. We recorded so many shows that I could choose performances that I felt were as good or better than the recorded studio versions, or where there was a level of live excitement, or where there was something genuinely new that was brought to the version, as opposed to just the best possible available to me. *Animate*, for example, evolved into something different live. So it was a more ambitious mission or goal. But at the same time, I think we accomplished a very satisfying result. In terms of tinkering, there's really

none on this album. The whole purpose of this album was to record so many shows that we wouldn't have to do any."

Most definitely, hearing 2112 in its entirety is a **Different Stages** high point. "We changed a bit of the emphasis and changed the tuning of the song a little bit to give it a heavier feel," notes Geddy on the Big Brother-like classic. "But other than that it's a fairly accurate reinterpretation of it, 22 years later [laughs]. I was really pleased with the way that came out. It was really a lot more fun to play live than I ever thought it would be."

But for the most part, the band takes it as a point of honor to reproduce the songs fairly closely to the manner in which fans know and love them. "For most of our songs, really, we do stick to the arrangements," affirms Neil. "The arrangements are so carefully wrought that we're quite happy to try to nail that on the night, you know? And other ones are a little looser by design. There's also a consistency of live performance that is really important to us. I always remember seeing The Grateful Dead around the early '90s. I had liked Mickey Hart's book, **Drumming at the Edge of Magic**, and I had written him a letter of appreciation, and we corresponded a little. And we were in Atlanta one night with back-to-back nights off, so I went to see Grateful Dead, and Mickey said right away, 'Well, it's not going to be very good tonight, because we just had a good show last night' [laughs], 'and they come in fours.' And that was

the kind of inconsistency that their approach to performance demanded and their audience would forgive. So, fine. We really like a lot more given consistencies so every night is going to be good. And if we happen to be sparked up, there's always room for that to show. And we notice a difference, and our audience notices the difference when it's a special night."

And, on a more micro level, Peart sticks to the original studio structures of most of his drum fills as well. "I do, with pleasure, yeah. Again, I worked really hard on all that stuff, and it's a reflection of me and my character, how I like to see things built, and the way I like to play, so why wouldn't I? It just seems obvious. There are always little details that I hear in the final record, and I go, 'I wish I knew that that accent or that vocal push was going to be there.' Because things get built and developed along the way. So, yeah, there are little things like that I've added afterwards, that I wished I had done on the record. But they are small details." And, in the end, I suppose there are all those air drummers you have to satisfy. . . . "Well, they can do what they want. No, no, that's strictly about me. The drum parts are made to suit me, and consequently they're played to suit me."

Yet ultimately there's a philosophical dissatisfaction, or deficiency, with the concept of getting out there and playing live versus the permanence of a record that you can hold in your hand. "Well, yes, that's the

distinction," affirms Neil. "Between temporary and permanent. In some ways, touring is an important evolutionary part of your progress, for sure, in that I used to definitely feel at the end of the tour that I was playing better and that the band was playing better than we had been at the outset. And as you're learning and growing and refining technique and all those different aspects of being a musician, there's no greater testing ground or proving ground than by performance, where you're proving yourself every single night.

"And again, playing the same songs but trying to correct flaws, or improve bits of it, get inflections, pick up what the other guys are playing, and incorporating that, listening to live tapes after the show, hearing where you might have nailed the tempo down better, or where you are playing something somebody might respond to. So many things like that go on in the course of touring, and again, especially in the early years, where things were accelerated and there's so much to learn, so you learned faster. Then it reaches a certain point, I find, where it's just re-creation.

"I love rehearsing for the tour and the whole buildup for it and the band becoming tight musically and working and all of that, right through the rehearsals and everything. Then once you've played a really good show, that sets the benchmark that you struggle to live up to night after night. And then, of course, if you do play a really great show, I've

had this experience of coming off stage all exuberant after a great show, and then a cloud of disappointment sets in, like, 'It's gone [laughs]. It's over.' So increasingly that becomes less satisfying.

"I think, to painstakingly craft a piece of work, whether it's writing or music or drumming, particularly, it's done, and it's there, and you can enjoy it later. It has a sense of not only endurance but accomplishment, like you've made something. A show doesn't feel like you've made something. That's the difference. You performed something, and it can be satisfying or not, depending on how well you performed it. But in essence, hey, you haven't actually made anything."

And the reverse? What do you get out of seeing a band live? "I would say it's more of a theatrical experience, really, for me," responds Neil. "I don't find that live performance has ever really changed my experience of music. Everything I get out of music I can get from the album. I love to go see a band perform, of course, but that's the essence; it's performance, it's the theater, the same way I like to watch a good play or opera. It's that kind of experience, I think, more than the intimate experience of music that you can have with speakers or headphones or in the car."

Back to Rush's own stages, Geddy addresses the topic of his understated, some say meekly delivered, stage patter. "I'm not a big talker on stage. Over the years, I've loosened up a lot; I feel much more comfortable. When I was young, I think I was just nervous. But as I've gotten older, it's much less of a big deal to me. When I talk, I feel totally at ease. But I don't remember, unless somebody threw a shoe or something at me, getting

pissed off and yelling at the audience [laughs]. There's the occasional time where you're in a general admission situation and people are shoving too much and you have to talk about calming everybody down."

"Geddy was the one who always spoke, and he spoke very little," notes Alex, who increasingly has taken to cracking spontaneously not a minimal quantity of quips, jokes and impressions on any given night. "You know, other than just introducing the songs, that was it. He was never the kind of host to the evening that some people are. It was all about getting down to business, playing. And I guess that's the way it always was with us. We never worked out moves. You just reacted to the music whatever way you did, and everybody was very independent."

The resplendent triple-gate packaging of **Different Stages** contains a nice collage of Rush memorabilia. "It's stuff from all of us really," says Geddy, "and some fans, I think. Our photographer, Andrew MacNaughtan, put the collage together. I keep stuff; I can't say I display much of it, but, yes, I'm a bit of a packrat. When I see things I think are cool, I throw them in a box and put it in the basement somewhere."

Finally, **Different Stages** adds yet another bonus, a computer program, Geddy explains, that allows the purchaser to indulge in musical sculpture. "Someone at Atlantic phoned me and said that they had got in contact with this Japanese artist who had developed this interesting program called ClusterWorks, and there was something about the program that they were anxious to use on a rock album. And something reminded him of the kinds of things we do with our lights and our live situation, with our lasers and so forth. So he thought there was a nice fit between our music and the ethereal quality of these visuals. He flew down and showed it to me. And I've never been a big believer in the enhanced CD thing, because in the past you always kind of get lyric sheets and things like that, so they make you feel like you're getting a bonus when you're getting things you normally would get anyway [laughs]. So I never really thought it was much of a bargain for the fans. But this struck me as being something different, and I imagine that there are a lot of fans who want to play with that. So, for those who want to play with it, it's there."

Vapor Trails

Almost exactly two years after the Different Stages live opus, Geddy released a solo album called My Favourite Headache. In an interview with me for that record, Lee mentioned plans about getting together with Rush again for a new studio album or at least a tour. In the meantime, he said, Alex was doing some producing and writing for TV.

Of the solo record, Geddy offered that "this record for me is very rewarding on two levels. One, I'm very proud of it musically, and two, I'm very pleased to be able to have worked with Ben Mink, who has been my friend for a long time. The whole reason this project came into being was my desire for the two of us to work together. And for us to work together and still remain friends at the end of it was a big accomplishment, I think [laughs]. I'm really happy about that. But musically the album is quite richly layered in terms of melody compared to where I normally operate. And it's a slightly different attitude toward groove in rock. It's a little rounder groove-oriented music than what we end up doing in Rush. Lyrically, I guess after I got over the original shyness about it, it turned out to be a very rewarding personal experience in terms of getting to know myself. It felt good to clarify my thoughts about certain things on paper. And the fact that they can translate into a musical world also made me feel more complete."

Vapor Trails, released in 2002, after a most circuitous path toward and arrival at maturity, would prove to be a very different kind of Rush album. Alas, it is a record that is rough, frazzled, fuzzy, noisy, claustrophobic, laden and leaden with meaning. Its making was and its being is revolutionary with respect to the code of ethics the band had fine-tuned over the course of 28 years. Central to Neil's recent life experiences, his travels, and his book of the same name is the track *Ghost Rider*, a carafe

splashing one of Rush's greatest examples of passionate melody. *How It Is* nudges cloud-burstingly a close second. Album opener *One Little Victory* would also be the lead single. Beginning with an amusing percussion barrage, the song quickly gets down to rocking out. The highly textural *Secret Touch* and the bog-blasted *Earthshine* would also become key radio tracks. *Peaceable Kingdom* and *The Stars Look Down* are trashy and combative, oddly evoking a bunker mentality one doesn't usually get from Rush's expansive ambitions. And the title track is sheer manic, chaotic, spiritual musicality — messy like life.

"Well, it's important to clarify in the beginning," says Alex on coming up with such a bewildering stew of stirred exotics. "We would only take four to six months to make a record, six being really the outside. To spend 14 months on a record is a long, long time. But Geddy, after spending a year on his solo record, really believed that we shouldn't have any deadlines. We've always been very anal about the way we work; you know, six weeks for writing, one week for drums, five days for bass, two weeks guitar, two weeks vocals, mix. It's always been like that.

"We've been doing that for decades, and with his solo record Geddy said, 'I played so much with my songs, and I could really see how they developed and how important it was to the growth of the material.' He said with **Vapor Trails** we had to do the same thing, not worry about deadlines, take as long as it takes to work that way.

"I was antsy for the first couple of months; I had that four-month to six-month thing in my head, and it was three months before we even had anything written. By that point, I realized that he was right, forget deadlines, this record is going to take as long as it takes. Even *Earthshine*, which was the first song we wrote, was completely rewritten. Even the lyrics were changed around. Musically, it was a completely different song from what it was, and it was a complete song in the beginning. We had all the parts, the lyrics, we worked it out, it was there. But there was something about it that just didn't knock us out."

"It's one of my favorite records that we've ever done," begins Geddy, who speaks in the spirit of confusion that **Vapor Trails** elicits in its listeners. "There's something about that record that is really raw and really passionate. And in some ways, even though it's nothing like it, it has a kind of focus that reminds me of **2112**, in a way, just in its kind of balls-to-the-wall attitude, the playing. It's a real album of playing out.

"Alex and I really wrote a long time. The first stuff we wrote was not very good. And we threw a lot of stuff away. But I think we almost needed to write a practice album before we got to the real one. It had been so long, so many years, since we'd written together. But we had to get a lot of stuff out of our system, shake off the rust. But when we finally started getting to the good stuff, a lot of it was just jamming, playing, that we recorded. We just left the machines running and

recorded it and shaped the songs out of that spontaneous performance. And I think we learned a really important lesson from that, something about . . . you have to really respect a performance and especially one that is improvised. And I think a lot of the spirit of that record comes from the fact that some of those are the original jams. A lot of those songs, or the final guitar parts and bass parts, were just things we had jammed together. There's a real honesty about it."

Alex charts the long, nearly imperceptible path that led to **Vapor Trails**, ending at the same place where Geddy started off. "**Counterparts** was great because it was the first record where we really stayed away from keyboards. We used very little keyboards, and of course that led eventually to **Vapor Trails**, which has no keyboards on it at all. And, I mean, that was my ultimate goal [laughs], to get to that point. I thought it was time for the guitar to take more of a prominent role in terms of those sorts of parts where we were using keyboards for, for pads, for atmospheric stuff. Why not create that on the guitar? Or vocals? Geddy knew that I had concerns about keyboards for a long time, and, like I say, over the last couple of records we've been using them less and less and less. They only appear as a backdrop and not like they were. With this record, we really wanted to make it more organic, more three-piece, more what we are. Ged was open to that, which was great. It gave me the opportunity to explore areas of the guitar that I could use for textures, the sorts of things that the keyboards used to do in the past. And I love

that; it's fun to make that instrument sound unlike what it's supposed to sound. And that's really what we did with **Vapor Trails**. It's always the most recent record that sits best with you, but even trying to be as objective as I can it's probably my favorite record that we've done."

Still, as Alex explains, the record emerges as downright inscrutable with respect to its relationship with the guitar. "The direction that I really wanted to go in for this record was a very anti-rock-guitar direction. Geddy plays a lot more chordal stuff, and that comes from his solo record. He wrote a lot of those songs on bass. You play chords to sing along to; he naturally gravitated towards that style, and when he would do things like that it took me somewhere else. I could play single-note lines, play more of a bass part when he was playing more of a rhythm guitar part. So we were changing roles, and that interested me; I really like trying to go in through the back door if I can. For me, what was important was to get the guitar to sound dissonant at times, and very rich harmonically, with a lot of noise going on in the background of whatever the melody was, counterpoint as much as possible to what Geddy was playing and sometimes to what Neil was playing, not only in terms of rhythm, but also in terms of texture and melody. And *Peaceable Kingdom* is one of my favorites because I think that's a great example of all those different elements, of shifts in tempo and shifts in rhythm and of melody.

"For the last five years, I've been playing a lot. I have a studio at home, and I've been writing an awful lot. For me, it's like going to the gym; it's

all exercises. And I don't mean, when I say exercises, playing scales; it's exploring sound and what sound can do generated by a guitar. So for me it wasn't really so much challenging as it was liberating. It really gave me a chance to pursue the stuff I like to do. I like coming in the back door and creating weird things. There's a dissonance to a lot of this record that is very appealing to the ear. It sounds like three or four guitars when in fact it's only one or two.

"I don't solo nearly as much as I used to. I think I have a solo on just about every song on every record that we've made, but I've gotten out of that for some reason. I love soloing, and I think relatively and objectively I'm a good soloist when it comes to composition of solos. But for some reason on this record it just wasn't in my heart. There are a few, but I just didn't find it as important. I thought it would be great if those quote unquote solo sections were more a band solo section where we just get into an instrumental thing and we're all grooving and playing off each other; that was far more satisfying.

"This was a great platform for exploration for me. The guitars are loud on this record for sure, and everything is. The bass is loud, the drums are loud, the guitar is loud. We managed to capture that, and that's really what our goal was from the beginning. I tried to create guitar parts that were simple yet sounded more complicated or complex than they really were. I really got into this idea of a guitar dissonance and playing across keys using keys that are usually against the wall and creating tension that way. Geddy's playing a lot of bass chords lately, and on

this record they become a little more dominant with all this other guitar noise in the background. To me, it created a sense of depth and greater dimension by doing that.

"There was a whole different mentality as we went into this project versus **Test for Echo**," explains Alex when asked to address the album's nervy production tones. "We were coming out of a dark period for the last five years. We make decisions about production very early on. We decided we were going to produce the record ourselves, as much as we could. And despite not really having a direction when we started, it came after a while, and once it did it had an energy of its own. This project I would have to say was more intense, even though the schedule was much more relaxed. **Test** was very much like the records in the past where we worked it up in a working environment, did preproduction, rehearsed it, basically learned it, then went into the studio and recorded the whole record. Whereas this record was just an evolving, growing, living thing throughout the whole process. As Geddy's said, a lot of the performances on the record were those initial jam performances. You know, they've been played once. Almost all of *Peaceable Kingdom*, for example, is from that one jam that we did; then we made the song up from that, added a couple little embellishments, the drums of course. But basically guitar and bass are from that one time; that's the one time it was played. I really love that idea."

Asked to clarify if this means that much of the record falls out of a "live arrangement" situation, Alex says, "Well, I wouldn't say almost all of them, but at least half, in terms of performance. Generally, Geddy and I would jam for three days. And then we would spend a couple of days compiling, weeding out the crappy stuff from what we thought was good, and then from there we would start assembling songs. The deal was, if we could better the performance, great, if we can't, fine. And songs like *Peaceable Kingdom* had a certain feel and energy to them. You know, you get into the studio and start playing, and you start thinking about it too much; everything is like that. And it becomes a little safe. When you're not thinking and just playing, it's coming from a different place, and you don't care, and it just goes. And it's a beautiful reflection of where you're at that very moment. That's what I love about it.

"That was definitely Paul Northfield," says Alex on the subject of the record's warm drum sound. "Paul came into the project about six months after we began. We recorded almost everything in the style that I just explained. We had a couple of songs that we still weren't too sure about in terms of arrangement, and Paul really had an objective ear. He really helped out a lot in fine-tuning some areas of the songs that we were a little unsure of, having lived with them for so long. We went to Reaction Studio, which is not known for its live room, as a drum room. It's actually quite a dead room. It's actually a jazzy room, very dry. Paul came in and just built it up to his specs — drywall everywhere. Every open space he could find was redrywalled. He really brought a lot of life to the room, and I think he did a really great job on the kit. The kit sounds to me very immediate. It really sounds like you're there in the room, which is not an easy thing to do."

Alex addresses the topic of Neil's intense yet eerily spare lyrics. "Obviously, having gone through what Neil went through, and what we all went through, it was definitely going to impact where this record was going to go. To me, the record is very optimistic. It's all about recovery and about hope, about a future, rebirth and moving forward. There are some dark moments, some sad moments, but generally it's really about those things that I just mentioned. And the course that the lyrics take to get that message across covers a lot of ground, from a very personal experience to a more universal representation of it. And Geddy and Neil worked very, very closely on getting that idea across. Neil has always been, I think, a writer who has written from an observer's point of view. He doesn't dictate one way or another, but he lets his feelings out, and they are taken in a universal manner. With this record, it was a very personal experience, and they worked closely together so the idea that Neil was trying to get across could be presented by someone else, in this case by Geddy — he has to sing the lyrics with conviction. So they worked very closely, and it was very professionally done. There was no question of a personal thing in it. It was more about what the best way was to get this across.

"It was cathartic for Neil," adds Alex candidly. "When we started in January of 2001, he drove back from his place in Quebec, along the same

route where his daughter had the accident. As he approached Toronto, it was a gray, January, late-afternoon/early-evening kind of day. The city's gray, it was rainy and slushy and the weight of everything just became too much. That was difficult for him — just that one thing — and that was before we even started working. He had to work very hard to build up his strength, and we gave him lots of time and space and support, but it was really up to him to prove to himself that he could start his life over again; that's really what it was all about.

"By the end of the record, I won't say he was the same guy he was six years ago, but he was a lot stronger, he was a lot happier, he was more determined — he's a very determined, very strong person, but all of that strength and determination was shattered. He's in the process of rebuilding and starting his new life. If he doesn't want to talk to anybody, I can understand completely, because it's going to be very awkward. People are going to want to ask him questions about that, so they're going to avoid asking him if it's a weird issue, which it would be. So why bother? He's very private anyway, always has been. We talked about it before, when we finished the record, and he said to us, 'It's hard enough for me to even think about what happened, let alone talk to strangers about it, so please can I just not do that?' Of course, don't even worry about it, don't even think about it.

"I think **Vapor Trails** really requires four or five listens before you get a sense of what it's about and where it's going," sums up Alex. "It really requires a commitment from the listener to get into it. There's a lot of meat on dem bones. For us, that's what music is all about. In our music, we like to challenge the listener and make it so that every time you put it on you hear something else or you get a different emotional reaction to a song you didn't have before."

Hype was sky-high for the band's first tour in more than five years. Ticket sales were brisk, giving the band a glimpse of what can happen when you make yourself scarce, something they had only toyed with in the past, be that with touring, records or indeed even interviews. We must also remember that making yourself scarce can blow up in your face — you can be forgotten — and that emphatically didn't happen here. Remarkably, the **Vapor Trails** tour proved that Rush could be an arena-level headline act for an uncommon 20, 25 years, indeed for every tour in a row since (give or take) 1980 and really, with only moderate scarcity practiced, more like a gentle and relaxed elasticizing of its record-tour cycle beginning in the early '90s.

On the subject of playing big shows versus the grinding gigs of the club days, Alex offers the following observation. "You know, we played a small gig in Germany on the last tour. It was a 1,200-seater, a little kind of club thing. And people always ask that. 'Do you miss the old club days? Being right there with the audience?' And, no, I don't. We've been doing arenas for so long that that's where we're quite comfortable. And to us, that is an intimate setting. There's a greater sense of power, I think, in an arena. The lighting can be more dramatic; the smoke on stage can add a sense of mystery to what's going on."

Ultimately, Alex and the band saw a flurry of activity in all corners with the arrival of **Vapor Trails**. Rust had to be shaken off, a new show needed to be designed and, of course, many, many interviews had to be conducted to tell the world that Canada's prog icons were back. "It's a little overwhelming," says Alex. "We've always done a lot of press before a release, but the workload this time around is three or four times what it's ever been before. I think it's because we've been away for five years. Times have changed. The Internet has become so much more important, so there's a lot of website interviews that we do now. I think we've made a really good record, and people are either surprised by it or very interested in it, so it's just upped the amount of work."

Once the **Vapor Trails** tour — to many a fan's disbelief — started rolling, adulate Rush-starved crowds were treated to five tracks from the new record: *Earthshine*, *One Little Victory*, *Secret Touch* and, working sort of alternate nights, *Ceiling Unlimited* and *Ghost Rider*.

"Geddy and I sat down and listened to a lot of material," explained Alex at the time about coming up with a satisfying raft of songs. "We

decided that we wanted to shake up the set list, freshen it up, drop a lot of those songs that maybe a segment of our audience has gotten used to expecting and mix it up a bit — play songs we've never played before or haven't played in a long time. That required us to go through all the albums and listen to everything. We listened to **Caress of Steel**, **Hemispheres**, and, man, we hadn't listened to those records in a long, long time. And generally our feeling was that they held up pretty good. Our recollection of them was much different from what we discovered. **2112** has held up well; it was such a great period. There's a lot of anger in that record, and I think it stands up as an idea as well as a musical piece. **Hemispheres** was a transitional record for us, the last of those big-concept things that we did. There was always a question of whether it was a really great work of ours or maybe not such a great work of ours [laughs]. But I think it stood up musically. There are some songs that we can't get around, like *Tom Sawyer* or *Spirit of Radio*; they're great songs to play anyway, so that's OK. But some songs you do get quite tired of playing over and over. It would be nice to challenge ourselves a little more, particularly with the older stuff that we haven't played that was challenging to play even back then."

Further on the process of going back and listening to the old records, Alex says, "My recollection of it was that things were a lot smaller and more amateurish. When we listened to all of those old ones, **Fly by Night**, **Caress of Steel**, **Kings** particularly, **Hemispheres**, they stood up pretty well. There was great energy, power and spirit in the playing. When you listen to something that you did 25 years ago, and you haven't heard in 20 years, it can be an eye-opening experience. We felt a lot better about our catalog at that point. We realized that some of these songs

really improve with maturity. We'll approach and attack them a little differently than we did in our early twenties when we wrote these things. We'll definitely play them with a different sense of feel and rhythm."

In interviews at the time, Alex looked forward to specific situations and talked about the upcoming hometown dates. "Yeah, we're going to do the Molson Amphitheatre. Primarily this tour . . . it's the first time we've ever done a summer tour, so it's basically going to be the sheds until the fall, and then we'll do one leg of indoor shows. I'm looking forward to that because the Molson's gig is going to be outside, the middle of July; if it doesn't rain, it's going to be beautiful, and there's a little particular vibe to that whole thing. But at the ACC in the fall, it's going to be so much more visually dynamic and dramatic, I think. We're planning a lot of things for this tour, sonically and visually, a lot of great video stuff. We've been working with a couple of companies that are leading edge in animation, and they've got some great ideas. The stuff that we've seen has been mind-blowing, so we're really excited about that. The show's going to have a really fresh new look to it. Howard Ungerleider has been our LD, the lighting director, from the very beginning. He's got some great ideas for a new light system. Between rehearsals and all the production meetings, it's been hard to think about actually playing, but it's all going to be really worth it. I think the show's going to look great. I know once we get over all these hurdles of work and we get into playing again, you know, that first show, it's all going to click."

And click it did, Rush bringing out the cinematic experience in grand fashion, offering a symphony of images (main ones revolving around a dinosaur motif) to operate in synch with major and unmercifully regular pyro effects ("sweltering hot this last tour, I can tell you," laughs

Alex), not to mention a bank of white clothes dryers, the day's wash spinning around throughout the show. "George Steinert on our crew went out and got them," says Alex. "He sourced them down and kind of fixed them up a little bit, took the heating elements out of them so that they were working but not heating. And he installed aircraft landing lights in them so that, when you opened them up, they glowed. You had to put Canadian quarters in to keep them going. Every night we tried to have guests up on stage to pump quarters into the machines to keep them running." On the subject of domestic chores, Alex lets on that the kitchen was also very well equipped. "We brought our own chef out on tour. Our food was always fresh, organic. And we could tailor the menus to whatever we wanted individually. So it was great having him out."

Geddy offers a bit of color to the story of Rush's celebrated live film work, the **Vapor Trails** jaunt including the most extensive yet. "I have a group of animators I work with. Norm Stangl at Spin Productions here in Toronto has been my point man for over 20 years in terms of making weird animation and rear-screen stuff. And every year we try to do something different or try to invent some interesting effect or gag or something, and we've had a lot of fun designing different things. We usually use different stylistic animators every time out just so we get a different visual look. And it's really one of the most fun parts of my gig, and it's something I always look forward to in preparing for a tour, sitting down with new creative people and having one of these great meetings where we just throw around all kinds of whacked-out ideas.

"And this time I wanted to do something very fresh and very spontaneous. We were put in touch with this guy named Greg Hermanovic over at Derivative who has invented this touch software which is really very cool, which has allowed us to have an actual live VJ, kind of, on the road with us. And what we would do is design live concepts for about 15 different songs, and he would design elements that he would blend live

every night. Some of them would be purely abstract, some of them would be representational, and it really opened up a whole new area.

"And, as a result, no two shows were the same because Jim Ellis, who was our operator, had the ability to improvise on a nightly basis. And sometimes the combination would just be magic. But you could go to two shows, and they really wouldn't be the same, although the elements would be the same. Depending on how he was feeling it, and how the band was feeling that night, the show around us would vary. And of course the longer the tour went on, he would start throwing new ideas in, so the show kept growing visually. It was really fantastic, and I thought it just worked terrifically, better than I ever expected. It was a wonderful addition to the show and something I think we'll keep up on tours in the future."

Finally, Geddy adds flesh to the tale of the dinosaur, prevalent in the film of which he speaks and then in the packaging of the tour's subsequent live memento **Rush in Rio**. "In the original **Vapor Trails** design, Hugh Syme had one version of the cover, where on the back, very small in the corner, was this very tiny dinosaur, who was the cause of this great vapor trail. And when we were doing the preproduction for the tour, I was looking for animation ideas to use live. I wondered what it would be like to exploit that little dragon a bit more, turn him into a character, which people at Spin Productions developed into a full-blown character that we used during *One Little Victory* live. It was a cool, humorous way to use this dragon. So again, the dragon was picked on by Hugh to become the representative of the show in Rio, and of course he's got him dressed up like Carmen Miranda."

Bounding around America and Canada dramatically for five months, Rush would close the tour off on an extraordinary note — playing Brazil for the first time ever, three triumphant shows, the net effect captured on the aforementioned **Rush in Rio** CD and DVD, released to great acclaim in 2003, winning the Juno for best DVD in April of 2004.

"The live experience and the studio experience have always been two different things for me," says Alex, at this point looking back on the tour that was. "The kind of energy that is required in the studio is quite different from the live show. I think, looking back over the 30 years, the live part of the whole experience has kind of come full circle, the **Vapor Trails** tour in particular. We played the best we've played; we were really tight. The level of satisfaction on a night-to-night basis was the highest, I think, it's ever been. Very few shows are tens, but we had, I think, a lot of nines. And the energy level seemed to touch on an earlier time, I think.

I guess it might be because **Vapor Trails** was more of a three-piece kind of record, and we had come full circle in that respect.

"We brought some stuff back like *By-Tor* and *Working Man*. They were truncated versions of the originals, but they were pretty true to their original form. I would say that we've always prided ourselves on being close to the record but with that added element of it being live, with the energy that you create on stage. It was always a disappointment to me to go see my favorite bands and not hear the original versions of the songs. That always seemed like a bit of a cop-out to me. So, from an early point, we always wanted to reproduce what we did in the studio fairly faithfully. You know, we might have eliminated some of the keyboard stuff here and there, eliminated some of the vocal harmonies that Geddy does. I try to help out as much as I can in that department, and we do have some samples. But he really loves to layer his vocals, and he does a terrific job at that. But those are some of the things that are expendable live. I don't think they get missed given the energy of the live show.

"Certainly *Resist* was different on that tour," says Alex, "going from an electric version to an acoustic one; that's probably the most transformed song. We always wanted to do something acoustic, but we weren't quite sure. We always resisted the urge to do that. We didn't want to do an unplugged thing which always seemed so trendy. But we thought it would be a nice break in terms of the three-hour show; we thought it would be refreshing. Plus we thought it would give Neil, depending on its placement, an opportunity to catch his breath after his drum solo. And to do it with quite a dynamic shift. So we worked on sort of a folk version of that, and I thought we pulled it off well. We really enjoyed that; Geddy and I both had a lot of fun just breaking down for those few minutes."

Commenting on other particular tracks of the tour, Alex says, "I don't think we've played *Working Man* since about '76 or '77, so it was a real treat to bring that back. We weren't sure about it; it's such a simple, kind of straight rock song, but it ended up being a great opportunity to jam and to really play your heart out, for all of us. The same thing with *By-Tor*. Some of those '90s songs, they come and go. They'll come into the set for a couple of tours, and then they'll go, and something else will come in. *The Pass*, for all of us, is one of our favorite songs to play, if not our favorite song to play. And *Bravado*, the same thing, we hadn't played *Bravado* in a while, and bringing it back was a real treat, because it's got such a nice mood. *Cygnus* is not that difficult really."

"All the new material, generally, requires the most concentration," adds Geddy. "Because, as a bassist and a singer, those songs aren't as firmly

entrenched in my memory banks, so it usually requires a huge amount of concentration for me to remember to keep my bass lines grooving with the drums, to make sure I trigger all the samples with my feet at the right time and to sing in key. Even near the end of the 70-date tour, it's still a challenge. Songs like One Little Victory, Earthshine and Secret Touch are by far the toughest part of the show for me."

Doesn't the profusion of bass chords also add to the internal drama? "Yes, but that is not so much of an issue in and of itself. The issue is playing them, singing and triggering all at the same time. Some of those songs have very complex backing vocal effects, loops, that are put on synthesizer that I have to trigger at the right time, otherwise they sound fucked-up [laughs]. So I'm basically triggering some vocal effects while I'm singing, while I'm playing bass. So it's a bit complicated up there at times [laughs]. And if you can't hear it all, you're in big trouble. In terms of older songs, I think the highest one to sing is 2112, parts of it. That's probably the toughest vocal song. Red Sector A is one of those songs I love to play because it gives me a break from the bass, and I can just go over to the keyboard and get into a whole different realm. Plus I think it's a great textural change for us live. And it's just one of those songs that is just a perennial. But of the new ones, I think Secret Touch is my favorite song on the record, and I love playing it live. It's got a great intensity about it."

"We were doing Bravado and The Pass, and both of those are impossible for me to play without feeling the emotion of them," says Neil, offering

his perspective on certain high-water marks of the set list. "That's a nice thing. A lot of times it can be just a performance where it's 'Okay, here's the song I have to play, and all these elements of subtlety go into playing it well; so here's what I'm going to do.' Whereas other times I do get swept up into the song itself and hearing the lyrics and watching the response of people through that. That's another special thing about live performance, on the emotional side. Apart from the excitement and the cheering and the adrenaline reaction, when you see an emotional reaction to songs like that, and see people swept up in it — and feeling it yourself — that's kind of an underappreciated and unglamorous part of what live performance can be."

"Neil will practice for anywhere from 20 minutes to half an hour before the show, immediately before the show," offers Alex on the subject of gearing up for show day. "He has one of those little five-piece practice kits that's just pads. But he pounds the crap out of them, and that's his way of warming up. It's basically like him doing a drum solo for 20 minutes. He really plays hard on the thing. I like to do the same and warm up for a minimum of half an hour before the show. Depending on my mood, sometimes it's an hour. Geddy, not so much. I don't think I saw him practice once on the last tour before the show. Although toward the end of the tour he had some tendonitis in his hand, so I do remember, actually, him spending a little time just warming up his right hand."

Finally, I asked Alex if there were any instances on the tour when the band experienced a real musical breakdown due to miscommunication or what have you. "Not really. We wear in-ear monitors, so we're very aware of what's going on and where everybody's at in terms of train crashes, which is what we call them. But I can't really think of anything on the last tour. Although it does happen. I'd say it happens twice, maybe three times, over the course of the tour, where suddenly somebody does something, and everybody is lost, and it sounds like very outside jazz, and then it just immediately goes back to the song [laughs]."

Before we move on, I should mention that, while not part of any tour per se, Rush ended up playing to their biggest crowd ever eight months

after the end of the **Vapor Trails** jaunt. The occasion was the Toronto Rocks concert on July 30th, 2003, billed as an economic booster for a city reeling from a bad tourism season due to the outbreak of SARS and reduced travel in general since 9/11. Headlined by the Rolling Stones but with AC/DC receiving most of the effusive press, the day-long festival found 400,000 people tramping off to a retired military base amid perfect summer conditions. Rush played third to last — a 35-minute set — and were the hands-down hometown heroes, although the Guess Who (on just before Rush) were appreciated as well. Earlier in the day, the Tea Party played their well-known cover of *Paint It Black*, and amusingly Rush returned fire, with an impromptu and brief jazzy version of the poisonous Stones classic, segueing into the set closer, *The Spirit of Radio*. Rush's set proper, however, consisted of *Tom Sawyer*, *Limelight*, *Dreamline*, *YYZ*, *Free Will*, *Closer to the Heart* and *The Spirit of Radio*, in that order. The band looked impressive in black, and, yes, the dryers survived SARStock.

Rush
in Rio

Serving as a sense-overwhelming exclamation point to the Vapor Trails tour, but more so of the global phenomenon that Rush had quietly become (without trying, without asking, without touring), Rush in Rio would be a giddy celebration of the love of music, stuffed with energy into a triple album and double DVD.

Specifically, the package captured the mania of the band's three-night stand in Brazil. Bear in mind that Rush is a band that toured Japan once, did the hula in Hawaii twice, toured Europe with limited atlas-cracking imagination, hit Mexico for one show on the **Vapor Trails** tour — and that's it for globe-strobing. Also bear in mind that South America loves hard rock, heavy metal and progressive rock, being quite the hotbed of the two natural convergences of the three: power metal and progressive metal. Tucking Rush under the equator and under those flame-thrown conditions would prove explosive.

Geddy offers a glimpse of the machinations that take place to make something like this happen in the first place. "Usually, we get this kind of yearly request to go play the Rock in Rio festival, and that's in January. And every time they held one, and they've invited us, we've been either in the studio recording — and you can't just stop that and do a one-off gig like that — or we've been not on the road at the time or not working; it's just been bad timing all these years. And the promoter was just determined to get us there this year, so he kept negotiating with us and pleading with us to come down, saying, 'You have no idea of your popularity down here,' which of course was true. We had respectable record sales, but we didn't realize how much in those countries that the record sales can't be accounted for because there's such a huge counterfeit record market down there; you have no way of knowing what you really sell."

Surely, then, there must have been certain guarantees. "Oh, yeah, they promised us they'd pay us a certain amount of money per gig, and they'll pay for our expenses, and they'll send us the cash upfront. Our manager, being exceedingly xenophobic and paranoid [laughs], wanted to make sure all these things were in place before he sent us down there. That wasn't in question. And, in fact, I don't think we had much doubt about that, quite honestly. Because our agent down there is the same as our agent in Europe and the rest of the world, and he's very experienced. There's no way he's going to connect us with somebody there where we're not going to get paid; that wasn't really in doubt. What was in doubt was whether we were as popular as he said we were or whether they could actually provide the technical assistance we needed to put on the kind of show that we do. But I had talked to some friends of mine who had played down there in other bands, plus other managers and stuff. People have been doing gigs down there for quite a while, so really I don't think there was that much to fear."

The highlights of the **Rush in Rio** CD and DVD are many. The video is packed with behind-the-scenes stuff, including hotel footage and Neil's warm-up regimen, the involved and meticulous show setup, plus

travel shots. Musically, the package is of course most distinguished by the inclusion of **Vapor Trails** material (most of it more frantic and quicker than the originals), including *Earthshine*, *One Little Victory*, *Ghost Rider* and *Secret Touch*. Disc three of the CD is retro heaven (and funny as hell once Alex takes over the mic), ending off with "The Board Bootlegs," namely a slamming, highly electric version of *Between Sun & Moon*, recorded in Phoenix, and an intimate, new wavy *Vital Signs*, captured in Quebec City. *Driven* and *Resist* are included, the latter, as discussed, in gorgeous acoustic form. *Leave That Thing Alone* percolates madly, leading into Peart's solo extravaganza, now known as *O Baterista*. The crowd sounds like waves crashing ashore — that is, when they aren't singing every syllable and then some, which is seldom.

"YYZ, especially in Brazil, that was one of the audience highlights of the show," says Geddy, graphically illustrating the crowd's appreciation of receiving a visit from their heroes. "As soon as we started playing that song, that whole crowd started bobbing up and down in time with it. And at one point, they're waving their arms doing a 'We are not worthy' thing in synch [laughs]. And what was amazing about the Brazilian crowds, when we played some of our instrumental stuff, they would be singing parts, like a lyric part for it on top of an instrumental. I don't

know whether they were soccer chants or what. It was amazing to me that they were singing well and adding new parts to our instrumental stuff [laughs]. I was amazed at how young people were as well. There were so many young people and many really good-looking young women too, which was a pleasure to look at. That's always a nice surprise at a Rush show [laughs]."

"It's surprising how in tune they are with everything — all forms of music," adds Alex. "They don't speak a lot of English down there, yet the audience was singing the whole night. And they very easily sung along with songs from **Vapor Trails** as they did from **2112** or **Moving Pictures**. I went down thinking that Brazil would be . . . not backwards, but, yes, lacking, but it was really the opposite. It's a very advanced culture. They've been around longer than we have. And I think in a lot of ways they are the pride of South America; certainly a city like Sao Paulo is, which is technologically advanced and is the center of commerce and technology for Brazil."

The band would play to 25,000 people in Porto Alegre, 40,000 in Rio, and an astounding 60,000 in Sao Paulo, making that show the biggest crowd Rush had ever played to as a headliner, next biggest outside the Brazil dates being far fewer, namely 20,000 at The Gorge in Washington state during the **Test for Echo** trek.

But technologically things didn't exactly go smoothly. "Well, there's a little more of that Latin influence," laughs Alex. "Things that we kind of consider important here — work, efficiency, those sorts of things — exist to a lesser degree there. Their priorities are more family, friends, having a good time, having a good meal, enjoying each other's company, much like it is going to Italy or Spain or something like that. We could learn a lesson from that."

Although the band played three shows, as Geddy explains, they wound up shooting only one. "It was a roll-the-dice kind of thing. It was actually the last show of the tour and not really our first choice. Originally, we were scheduled to shoot a show in the US, on the east coast. But at the last minute, there were problems with the venue, and it suddenly got canceled. And we just kind of said, 'Well, what are we going to do?' Because we had planned to do it as more of a high-definition photography experiment using really state-of-the-art gear. And then we changed to a completely different kind of video, and it was suggested, 'Why don't we shoot one of the shows in South America?' Because those shows will have more color and kind of a concept to it. Rather than just being the band performing in a technical environment, it will be this interesting slice of life. So we had to throw everybody into panic mode, such as the production house. And actually my brother, who is in the film

and various companies, took over as executive, kind of a production overseer, coordinating all the various departments. And they set up the production in Brazil, which was quite interesting [laughs], a combination of our own people and cameras and using what we could find there. There were over 20 cameras involved in the shoot.

"All hell broke loose every day there," recalls Geddy with a shake of the head. "You know, you never know what you're dealing with when you go to a country like that. When they ask, you tell them what you need technically, and they say, 'Oh, yes, we understand.' That doesn't mean you're going to have it [laughs]. That just means they understand what you want [laughs]. This was the fine line of semantics that we discovered. So every day there was a new surprise, in terms of the technical aspect of getting the show up, let alone 20 cameras and a recording truck. And the recording truck, by normal contemporary standards, was quite basic. And I think the same is true with a lot of the photographic equipment they were using. But they had some good cameramen, and they had a great director and really good crew and a lot of experience in the periphery. But again, you just never know what's going to happen.

"And on that particular day, we hadn't counted on it being such a circuitous route from Sao Paulo to Rio. It took the truck about eight hours to get there. And because the shows are so much later . . . I mean, we didn't go on in South America until 10:30. And we play a three-hour show, so do the math. And by the time you get the show down. . . . And of course for the show in Sao Paulo the previous night it was raining

throughout, so the gear was all wet. So it was a case of loading trucks in the middle of the night, in the rain, then driving eight hours. By the time they got the first piece of equipment on the stage, it was about two in the afternoon. We usually arrive at six in the morning, and the show is ready to go by six in the evening. So they were up against it, definitely."

"We had rain, actually, on the first two nights," adds Alex. "In Porto Alegre, which was the first gig in the south, it was raining hard. By the time we went on, it had stopped, but everything was wet. The stage was wet, our carpet was wet, some of the gear was wet. There was a problem with the console; it got wet. We managed to get it all going and working; it was a real miracle. The next gig in Sao Paulo . . . you know, we do a three-hour show, and we split it with a little intermission between the two sets. Towards the end of the first set, it started to rain. And during the second set, it rained. And I don't mean it rained on the audience, and we watched them get wet. It rained everywhere. And the wind was blowing towards the stage. So really, all of us, including Neil, were soaked — water just pouring off us.

"The advent of radios makes things a little less dangerous up there," explains Alex when asked if electrocution concerns might have stopped the show. "So you're not really worried about making a connection from one point of electricity to another — i.e., from the guitar amplifiers to the mic PA — so we just carried through. But toward the end of the set, my pedal board started to short out. Some of Neil's electronic kit started to short out.

"We made it through that set, and the following day, which was the following gig, in Rio, it was a long drive. They just started setting up when we would normally be doing our soundcheck. So no soundcheck, no line check, no video line check. There were problems with the power; requirements had not been met. There were problems with the staging. Everything that could go wrong did go wrong. The audio truck for the recording of the DVD [laughs] . . . boy, it was a relic from another era. Everything that could have gone wrong . . . the potential was there. And we managed to go on at 10:30, and the show went off without a hitch. The camera setup for the DVD all worked. It was amazing that we got away with it. All the equipment problems that we had the night before had miraculously sorted themselves out, thanks to our terrific crew."

Between the focal and vocal three, fortunately, not much went wrong either. "Well, Alex was having a problem with a cameraman in the first set, and he started freaking out at him, lost some concentration and had a gaffe in one of the songs, during one of the solos," says Geddy. "And after the set, we had to kind of cool him off and remind him that you've got to forget about that; you can't let those things bother you during a show that you're filming. Because there's just no sense looking pissed off on tape. He got the message, but it's very hard. There was so much going against us that day. We were going on cold; everyone was going on cold. And, to add to the confusion, there were all these extra lights that the camera people had put on stage without discussing with us. So there were these wires running across the front of the stage that were inhibiting our ability to go to the front of the stage and ham it up with the crowd kind of thing. And that was really disconcerting for me because I'm used to just roaming around and having some fun. And when I'd venture to the edges of the stage, I suddenly had to look at my feet to make sure I didn't trip over these stupid cables. The way you want to record a show should be ideal, and the last thing you should be thinking about is all this crap, so this was pretty fucked-up in terms of our ability to stay calm, cool and collected."

A question to Neil with respect to major mishaps he's experienced back there with his kit yielded the following early days story. "Well, everything's happened at one time or another. Certainly the worst is being on television. It must have been in '74, *In Concert* or *Rock Concert*, one of those shows, and . . . bass drum head. The ultimate worst thing that can happen. I think it's only happened to me twice ever, and one of them was on television in the middle of our performance, and we had to stop, of course, fix it and start again. So that's about as bad as it can get. Of course, it wasn't live television, so there is that. With snare heads, cracked cymbals, at least you can wait and replace them, but that still happens frequently enough. Everything else you learn how to work around. Except if the bass drum goes, that's a real fundamental thing. If a snare head breaks, I can use a high tom. I used to have a timbale; I can use a timbale as a snare for a while. And it was a nuisance and upsetting to the concentration and the flow — and a bad check on the performance.

"Every night I go on with a blank slate, and every song I go through, 'OK, that's one; OK, that's two. I played good, I played it good, nothing went wrong, I played it good.' There's that kind of scoreboard I go through every night. It's the tally against the perfect show. And again, I was talking to you before about the different ways of looking at touring at different points in your career. That's what it becomes for me now. And that's why it's so hard and ultimately so unrewarding. Because at best you get an average [laughs]. An E for effort; 'OK, that one is good.' And it really is like that. 'OK, we're halfway through, I'm still playing well, I haven't made any mistakes, still nothing's broken.'"

Neil then adds this instance from South America, illustrating the additional problems electronics bring to the game. "When we were in Brazil at the end of the last tour and we were about to film and record the very last show, the night before we got in a pouring rainstorm on stage, and it drenched the equipment, and some of my stuff wasn't working, and I was playing around it all that night. . . . If you consider the mental mechanics of playing the drums anyway, and then to be playing in two places, as it were mentally, of 'What I'll do, okay . . . what about when I get to that song? That's not going to work. What should I use instead for the electronic sound? And how can I cover up that?' And imagining my whole drum solo. At some other part of the set, I'm playing some other song, and then thinking ahead, 'OK, my drum solo; that's not going to work, so I'll do this and this and this.' It's restructuring in my head as I'm going.

"I've often said about drums, or probably any instrument, if you're not at least eight bars ahead of yourself, you are in trouble. If you have to think about what you're doing right now, you're probably in trouble. And it's that kind of distraction, when something goes wrong, that jars you. Suddenly, you're just thinking about where you are and keeping up with it. That's the kind of thing that upsets a performance and makes you less satisfied with it. But, yeah, in the general flow of things, I'm way ahead to the next transition, for instance, setting up mentally and physically, for moving into that flow and keeping its mood and nailing the tempo — all the tiny little things of technique. So that's all flowing through your head in the course of the show.

"So, yeah, if something has gone wrong, it affects everything; then you're completely and mentally just solving equations. I compare playing drums for Rush to running a marathon and solving equations at the same time. So when you're solving equations in real time and in future time also, it's not pleasant, you know? You can do it, and survive it, and 'Whew, we made it,' but it's not fun [laughs]! That's the only way to say it. It's not fun."

I wondered if, through all the chaos and activity, the band got to play tourist at all. "In Brazil, no, because it was always a whirlwind," says Alex. "We got down there, and there were a couple days off, but we were traveling around a lot. There was a lot of press to do. We always do a meet and greet before the show, sign a bunch of stuff, take pictures with fans. There was a very robust schedule for us in terms of the promoter and record company keeping us busy. And then we had dinners every night; they wanted to take us to all kinds of different restaurants and things like that. So we were kept pretty busy the whole time down there. But on the course of the **Vapor Trails** tour, yeah, I play a lot of golf; Geddy goes out and plays with me maybe half the time. We also play a lot of tennis. Ged likes to go to art galleries and movies. You know, just try to do normal stuff and keep busy."

"I think all of our wives came down," says Geddy of the trip to Brazil. "Pegi [Cecconi, important figure at Anthem and all-round Rush enabler] as well. We forced Ray to come on the whole tour, just to prove to him that it's OK to be in another country [laughs]. We had a lot of fun, and it was really a terrific time. The people in South America treated us very, very well."

On the subject of meeting the fans, Geddy confirms that Rush held meet-and-greets every night. "We posed for photos and signed autographs; there are contest winners. It's a very short 15 minutes, but we get all kinds, as you can imagine. We've got people who've named their children Alex, Geddy and Neil. Most of them are very hardcore fans who are just thrilled to have the opportunity to talk with you for a couple minutes. So it's kind of a sweet moment, and I don't mind doing it."

Extending that experience to all of the years, Geddy says, "I think we've signed everything from picture discs to baby pictures to women's breasts. You just never know what's going to be put in front of you to sign [laughs]."

Alex adds a comment on gifts the band's been given. "Some people have done some very big paintings, some small ones. You get some things that are almost like school projects that have diagrams and drawings, basing something on a song. Japanese fans would send paper fans, boxes

of incense. I remember getting an engraved glass goblet from a fan in Manchester, England. Um . . . I haven't seen anything lately. People are getting too cheap [laughs]." Another memorable gift was a set of dolls (this was in the early '90s, before Bobbleheads, of which a Rush set exists), which both the boys and the crew found a little eerie due to how much they looked like the guys.

Alex offers a few comments on the construction of the DVD. "Well, the DVD was a lot of work. When we came off the road, Geddy and I sort of decided that, if there were any kind of video decisions to be made, he would look after that. Any audio decisions that needed to be made, I would look after that. We started mixing it, and I thought I'd be in every other day for a couple of hours. I was in the studio every day from noon until four in the morning for eight weeks. So it was a lot of work. The original intention was just to do the 5.1 format, and then Atlantic decided they wanted to release the CD, so there was that added, and it was the whole show again, in a stereo version. The work just piled up and piled up. So I worked really hard that summer, a summer where I just expected to kick back. The previous two years had been very busy and very hectic for us, so it was nice to just kind of have that fall off."

The 30th Anniversary Tour

Which brings us to the here and now and a tour we can't fondly reminisce about over beers because, as I write, the band has not yet hit the trail. Rather, the guys are deeply ensconced in rehearsals for the 30th anniversary jaunt this book celebrates, a tour intended to hit many new corners of Europe. (You see? You can teach old snow dogs new tricks.) It's interesting, but before this tour's wheels were greased, the band reflected on their experience in South America in '02, wondering if it would be time to head back there again come '04. Indeed, Argentina and Chile were mentioned by Geddy, but as it stands there are no South American dates on the tour.

"At this stage, I'm not so sure," said a wary Alex in the interim about whether the blissful Brazil reception had opened doors and minds to hitting additional exotic locales. "If there was someplace we could go to where we could have the kind of response we had in Brazil — which, quite frankly, we had no idea we had that kind of popularity there — then it would be worth it. But at this stage in our career, to go to a country that is exotic, just to go there, and to play for a couple thousand people, is really not something we're interested in. Our show is big, it's costly, we don't like to compromise it, we don't like to do festival sorts of things. The occasional special event, yes, OK, but we like to be in control, and we like to present the band in a certain way. So it has to be the right place." In fact, it was touch and go whether Rush would tour at all, the band nearly deciding on making a new studio album instead. It is of no matter: the tour was to go ahead — and quite extensively at that.

"I know that this is a very unusual life to have led," says Alex, looking back at the drama and dreams fulfilled thus far. "And, you know, I've wondered for a long time, why is it that I'm blessed with this whole thing? Of course, what's happened in the last two months has sort of not been too much of a blessing. And of course with Neil too. But of course you're right, it is a very unusual and special gift, I think, that we've all been so generously given."

After talking with Alex about family and his wish — had he a chance to do it all over again — to have had four kids (he is, in place of that, a grandfather now and loving it), I asked him if, indeed, he could have given all of this rich creative life up for family. "You know, I don't know how to answer that question," he says thoughtfully. "Creativity is really important to me, but it's not the forefront of my head. When I sit down and do something creative, it's a powerful thing for me; it's physically powerful. I feel, well . . . different from normal, when I go through that kind of experience.

"For example, I have a studio, and my son writes electronic music, kind of trancy stuff. And last weekend, on Sunday, he wanted me to play guitar. We wanted to re-create a kind of a Middle Eastern flavor. So we used the banjo, and it sounds a lot like a guitar depending on how we tune it. And it's a weird tuning, so your head has got to get into that mode, and I just sort of got lost in it. We spent hours doing this stuff, and it felt like minutes! Everything was all over the place. The tuning was crazy, playing the banjo was not easy, but we got great stuff! It was really unusual. And at the end of the night, I was shaking, just from the excitement.

"And sometimes as I get older, I'm just not in that place as much. Whereas when I was younger, I was always in that place. But it was all part of my life, and I kind of took those things for granted. You know, I've always been a very go-with-the-flow kind of person. I've never been great on making plans and things like that. When we work, I'm the one who is spontaneous. My best work is in those first few takes. Geddy's the opposite. He likes to develop an idea, experiment, try everything before he makes his final decision on what he thinks is good about what he's doing. And his may be a more intelligent approach, whereas mine is more from the gut. And I think that's why we complement each other and work so well together. I think, if I didn't have that creative outlet, I would be very unhappy. But like I say, I don't really think about it. It's such a natural part of my life and who I am. And I guess that's because I've been allowed to have it that way."

One wonders how much longer we will actually see Rush heeding the call of the road. It's no secret that touring is especially hard on the system, especially when your spring chicken days coincided with the Carter administration. "I'm 50, and it's hard to lose weight!" laughs Alex, truly but only moderately surprised. "Really, really hard. I've been really good about eating. I don't eat any bread, potatoes, no real empty carbs. I used to think about losing weight, and I'd lose it — not anymore. I do yoga practice for an hour and a half once a week, and I try to do a couple other days, but generally it's just that once a week. I work out at a gym twice a week. I do at least two tennis clinics; one is two hours, one is an hour. I try to play every other day. You know, I'm doing a lot! [laughs]. And it's not budging.

"But I feel better, I feel stronger, and it's important to get into shape for the tour. You really feel it out there, not so much in the first month or two months, but after that it's a real curve. You just get tired; you don't have the same level of energy. It's difficult to travel, and your hours are screwed up. You get into that two or three o'clock in the morning slot where you're going to bed. And I hate . . . I can't sleep in anymore. On the road, really, the first half of the tour, I'm up 6:30, 7:00. I like getting up early, especially in the summer. And again, I try to do my yoga on a daily basis on the road. And I love playing golf, all that stuff. Then halfway through the tour, that catches up to you. And by the end of the last tour, I was sleeping until 11:00. You're out of gas."

Still, Alex, Neil and Geddy are, for all intents and purposes, in damn good shape. They all have their sports, and that fact of wider life — and no doubt the feeding of their minds as well — have been reflected in their sturdy statures. By maintaining balanced lives, they've managed to keep themselves steadily rocking through four different decades. Indeed, it's been inspiring to see them add what can only be assumed to be yet another career plateau, the Brazil experience, only so recently.

"Well, that too tends to be a progressive, linear thing," opines Neil on that subject. "When I was a kid, I thought that playing at the roller rink would be the greatest thing ever. And then coming up, Massey Hall; the idea of growing up in St. Catharines and coming to concerts at Massey Hall . . . what could be greater in the universe than to play at

Massey Hall? So those were early unrealistic dreams more than goals. I think of it long-term.

"But, yes, Radio City Music Hall is of course a magical experience. The first time, going back to England and playing the Hammersmith Odeon, that was huge at the time and still, in retrospect, shines, as kind of a magic nexus of time and place. But, hey, a lot of great shows have happened, at Knickerbocker Arena [laughs] or a theater in Oklahoma City or a club in Corpus Christi. Those things aren't identifiable as place. But, yeah, those kinds of ones can't be forgotten.

"I'm looking forward to doing the Hollywood Bowl, for example, this summer, just for the historic nature of it — and the novelty of it; let's face it. So many of these places in North America, the arenas and the amphitheaters, we've been to so many times. For years, I rode my bicycle to them, and now I ride my motorcycle to them. I know exactly how to get there and what roads they're on and what entrance to go in and all that stuff. So it becomes comfortingly familiar. It is nice to go to a place you know of, the backstage area; you know where the dressing rooms are, where everything is. There's something nice about that, but of course novelty is exciting too after 30 years of traipsing around."

Finally, I had to ask Neil if through those 30 years any bouts of interpersonal craziness, perhaps beginning with fan interactions, stick out in his mind. His searching pause and then succinct answer provide a sense that there are just too many to mention. "Psychotic fans, yes. All the time

— constantly. That's a reality of life. It's not remarkable, I have to say. To be surrounded by craziness, by organized crime, by union corruption and by corruption of all kinds throughout the music industry, record companies, radio stations . . . I mean, it's a part of these times, so consequently it's a part of our lives."

In closing, given that theirs has been a kaleidoscopic journey of extensive live work, and that ours has been a nostalgic discussion of the same, I wondered what thoughts were coursing through their minds as the band would soon set foot on stage after 30 years of bringing their unique form of mystic, rhythmic, natural science to the masses. "You know, we started the band 35 years ago," reflects Alex. "It's second nature with us; I mean, it's what we do. Going on stage, for all of us, our heads are in performance mode. When you're playing, it's down to business. For us, there's not a lot of room where you cannot be concentrating; you're really inside of what's going on. It's very busy on stage, and I find that, if you get into the zone, then you're fine. You can sort of sit on top of it.

"But there are distractions, technical problems, in which case it's very difficult to keep up the concentration. But in terms of the audience and those other sorts of external thoughts, you leave them for other times. Instead, you're thinking about where you're maybe speeding up in a certain song or things to look out for from the last gig. We tape every show, so we're constantly updating what's happening with the show. So I guess our approach is a very professional and performance-oriented process before we go on.

"And then other times you go on and think, 'Wow, I can't believe people are paying me to do this.' It's just such a joy, and it's so much fun. Particularly, the last tour was great. We had an amazing time. I thought I played really, really well, and the response was terrific. It was nice to do a summer tour. We had never done a summer tour before. In fact, we had come off five very difficult years where we weren't even sure we were going to tour again, which made it that much more special. I don't think we took a single moment for granted."